Strategic Management in the Community College

Gunder A. Myran, *Editor*

NEW DIRECTIONS FOR COMMUNITY COLLEGES
Sponsored by the **ERIC** Clearinghouse for Junior Colleges
ARTHUR M. COHEN, *Editor-in-Chief*
FLORENCE B. BRAWER, *Associate Editor*

Number 44, December 1983

Paperback sourcebooks in
The Jossey-Bass Higher Education Series

Jossey-Bass Inc., Publishers
San Francisco • Washington • London

EDUCATIONAL RESOURCES INFORMATION CENTER

ERIC Clearinghouse For Junior Colleges

UNIVERSITY OF CALIFORNIA, LOS ANGELES

Gunder A. Myran (Ed.).
Strategic Management in the Community College.
New Directions for Community Colleges, no. 44.
Volume XI, number 4.
San Francisco: Jossey-Bass, 1983.

New Directions for Community Colleges Series
Arthur M. Cohen, *Editor-in-Chief*; Florence B. Brawer, *Associate Editor*

New Directions for Community Colleges (publication number USPS 121-710)
is published quarterly by Jossey-Bass Inc., Publishers, in association with
the ERIC Clearinghouse for Junior Colleges. *New Directions* is numbered
sequentially—please order extra copies by sequential number. The volume
and issue numbers above are included for the convenience of libraries.
Second-class postage rates paid at San Francisco, California, and at additional
mailing offices.

The material in this publication was prepared pursuant to a contract
with the National Institute of Education, U.S. Department of Education.
Contractors undertaking such projects under government sponsorship
are encouraged to express freely their judgment in professional and
technical matters. Prior to publication, the manuscript was submitted
to the Center for the Study of Community Colleges for critical review and
determination of professional competence. This publication has met such
standards. Points of view or opinions, however, do not necessarily represent
the official view or opinions of the Center for the Study of Community
Colleges or the National Institute of Education.

Correspondence:
Subscriptions, single-issue orders, change of address notices, undelivered
copies, and other correspondence should be sent to Subscriptions,
Jossey-Bass Inc., Publishers, 433 California Street, San Francisco
California 94104.

Editorial correspondence should be sent to the Editor-in-Chief,
Arthur M. Cohen, at the ERIC Clearinghouse for Junior Colleges,
University of California, Los Angeles, California 90024.

Library of Congress Catalogue Card Number LC 82-84179

International Standard Serial Number ISSN 0194-3081

International Standard Book Number ISBN 87589-942-0

Cover art by Willi Baum
Manufactured in the United States of America

This publication was prepared with funding from the National Institute of
Education, U.S. Department of Education, under contract no. 400-83-0030.
The opinions expressed in the report do not necessarily reflect the posi-
tions or policies of NIE or the Department.

Ordering Information

The paperback sourcebooks listed below are published quarterly and can be ordered either by subscription or single-copy.

Subscriptions cost $35.00 per year for institutions, agencies, and libraries. Individuals can subscribe at the special rate of $25.00 per year *if payment is by personal check.* (Note that the full rate of $35.00 applies if payment is by institutional check, even if the subscription is designated for an individual.) Standing orders are accepted. Subscriptions normally begin with the first of the four sourcebooks in the current publication year of the series. When ordering, please indicate if you prefer your subscription to begin with the first issue of the *coming* year.

Single copies are available at $8.95 when payment accompanies order, and *all single-copy orders under $25.00 must include payment.* (California, New Jersey, New York, and Washington, D.C., residents please include appropriate sales tax.) For billed orders, cost per copy is $8.95 plus postage and handling. (Prices subject to change without notice.)

Bulk orders (ten or more copies) of any individual sourcebook are available at the following discounted prices: 10–49 copies, $8.05 each; 50–100 copies, $7.15 each; over 100 copies, *inquire.* Sales tax and postage and handling charges apply as for single copy orders.

To ensure correct and prompt delivery, all orders must give either the *name of an individual* or an *official purchase order number.* Please submit your order as follows:

Subscriptions: specify series and year subscription is to begin.
Single Copies: specify sourcebook code (such as, CC8) and first two words of title.

Mail orders for United States and Possessions, Latin America, Canada, Japan, Australia, and New Zealand to:
Jossey-Bass Inc., Publishers
433 California Street
San Francisco, California 94104

Mail orders for all other parts of the world to:
Jossey-Bass Limited
28 Banner Street
London EC1Y 8QE

New Directions for Community Colleges Series
Arthur M. Cohen, *Editor-in-Chief*
Florence B. Brawer, *Associate Editor*

Contents

Editor's Notes

Remember the old saw about how difficult it is to remember that your mission is to drain the swamp when you are up to your waist in alligators? Most community college managers can probably identify with that dilemma. It is hard to spend time on long-term planning and college development when you are under daily pressure to deal with a myriad of crises, deadlines, complaints, projects, and meetings, yet there is a growing sense that a transformation — perhaps one could even call it a revolution — is taking place in community college management. The transformation involves a shift in emphasis from operational to strategic management, from running a smooth ship to steering the ship.

Why is this transformation taking place? What is wrong with our stereotype of the college dean, wearing a tweed jacket with patches on the elbows, sitting with pipe ablaze and feet propped up on a desk in contemplation of the latest proposal to change degree requirements? Well, there is probably nothing wrong with the dean, but the stereotype is to a great extent an anachronism. In the long-lost past, an excellent faculty member became a dean without any management training or background. In fact, any suggestion of business or management orientation would have violated the sensibilities of many college staff members. The basic management philosophy was, If it ain't broke, don't fix it. The college was isolated from the realities of life on the street corner, in the factory, and in the home. Any economic or social change in the external environment that required the college to adapt happened slowly enough that no sophisticated management or planning process was needed to bring about needed internal changes.

This idyllic circumstance shattered in the social revolution of the 1960s. The pace of social and economic change accelerated, and the old mechanisms — the faculty senate, the president's cabinet, student government — were found wanting. The issues to be dealt with were no longer degree requirements, new courses, or the annual awards dinner but rather fundamental future-oriented issues about who should be served, what the scope of programs and services should be, and where programs should be located. The colleges were dragged into the future by climactic social events. A frenzy of change occurred as the community colleges reached vertically into the social structure to serve groups that had been systematically excluded from access to higher education in the past and horizontally across the social structure to take on new social roles and new educational responsibilities.

A transformation from the campus-based to the community-based college was dramatically under way, and sometimes the colleges stretched too far or promised too much. They found that they could not be the knight in shining armor who charged forth to cure all social ills. But, charge they did, and change they did. In the process, a new generation of community college managers emerged. Their titles included such terms as *minority services, community services, public relations, business and industry services,* and *women's resources.* These positions symbolized a new externally oriented management style that was replacing the traditional internally oriented style.

Even as the social revolution of the 1960s was cresting, the transformation from an industrial to an information society was gaining momentum. One characteristic of the transformation was its rapidity. The change in so many economic, social, and political arenas was so rapid in the 1970s and early 1980s that it became difficult for community colleges to determine which external stimuli to respond to; thus, it became very important to develop systematic ways of assessing opportunities and threats in the environment and establishing priorities among all the possible responses that a college could consider. To meet this need, community colleges began to employ professional planners and to develop comprehensive long-range and short-range planning systems. These planning systems, which are now in place in perhaps 10 percent of all community colleges, have solved some of the problems. In order to function in a turbulent and rapidly changing environment, community colleges have begun to emphasize a more systematic approach to establishing relationships in the external environment; for example, with potential student constituencies, business and industry, labor, government units, other educational institutions, the religious community, social agencies, and community service groups. These colleges have begun to place more emphasis on integrating the community-responsive thrusts and initiatives of the various college divisions and programs into a cohesive institutional mosaic. They have begun to devote more time and energy to strategy formulation and implementation; that is, to charting out definite courses of action that will shape the fundamental character and direction of the college. It is this combination of relationship building, assessment, strategic formulation, and strategic implementation that is referred to as *strategic management.*

The transformation from operational to strategic management will be one of the major phenomena within community colleges during the coming decade. On a functional basis, strategic management will have an impact on all areas of college functioning:

- Development of college philosophy and mission: activities that create and articulate the basic values and beliefs on which the college is founded and that describe the basic purposes and social roles of the institution
- Strategic planning: research and decision making that relates to assessing opportunities and threats in the external environment, auditing internal strengths and weaknesses, establishing long-range institutional goals that match external and internal conditions, and adapting long-term courses of action that shape the fundamental character and mission of the college
- Financial resource development and allocation: activities and systems that match the college's financial resources with its mission and long-term goals, improve the quality of strategic decisions made by users of financial information, and create an effective structure of financial management
- Program and service development: the structure of activities that identifies the changing educational needs of the community and creates and modifies the college's programs and services
- Development of administrative and program structures: activities in which the administrative structure and the structure of the college's instructional programs and services are established, evaluated, and modified
- Staff development: activities that determine the structure within which recruitment, selection, orientation, and in-service training take place
- Campus development: activities that create a long-range plan for the development of college facilities and grounds and ensure that adequate funds are available for such development
- Internal communications and working relationships: activities that involve all staff and student groups in the governance of the college and attend to the quality of work life within the college
- External relations: the structure of activities that creates the public image of the college and that establishes the relationship between the college and citizens, businesses, legislators, government officials, community leaders, potential students, and other groups external to the college
- Quality assurance: the structure of activities designed to assure quality, including program evaluation, evaluation of

administrative functions, staff evaluation, general and specialized accreditation, and institutional research

- Functioning of the governing board: activities designed to ensure the effective functioning of the governing board, including the development of college policies.

This sourcebook emphasizes six strategic areas: external relations, internal communication and working relationships, financial resource development and allocation, program and service development, staff development, and strategic planning. In Chapter One, Gunder Myran defines strategic management and demonstrates the need for strategic management in community colleges. In Chapter Two, James Gollattscheck indicates that external relationships are a major factor in determining the future of the community college. He demonstrates the need for high quality and in-depth relationships in the external environment of the college and describes the levels of relationships that can exist. In Chapter Three, Dennis Bila deals with the opportunities and hazards involved in creating effective future-shaping communications and working relationships within the community college. He describes the options available as a college makes the transition to a shared governance model and describes the possible involvement of staff unions in such a model.

In Chapter Four, Warren Groff explains the elements of strategic planning. He emphasizes the need for external assessment, internal audit, and goal setting. In Chapter Five, Albert Lorenzo demonstrates that the future of the community college is controlled by what it has the financial resources to be. He analyzes the utility of financial strategies, including pricing, diversification of revenue sources, and allocation and reallocation systems. In Chapter Six, George Baker and Kay McCullough Moore discuss the functions of program and service development and describe the strategic elements that can move dreams and goals to action and reality. They write of program and service development as a form of opportunism — taking advantage of opportunities and circumstances that can be shaped to the college's missions and goals. In Chapter Seven, Nancy Armes and Terry O'Banion focus on the role of the chief executive officer in strategic staff development. They emphasize the need for the community college president to have continuing opportunities for professional and personal growth if the college is to have strategies of quality and vision. In the final chapter, Jim Palmer reviews documents in the ERIC system that relate to strategic management in the community college.

Gunder A. Myran
Editor

Gunder A. Myran is president of Washtenaw Community College in Ann Arbor, Michigan, and an adjunct professor in the Center for the Study of Higher Education at the University of Michigan.

Those within community colleges realize that the future does not just happen; rather, creating the future starts in the minds and hearts of key decision makers, and it is given shape by their will and energy.

Strategic Management in the Community College

Gunder A. Myran

We marvel at the skill and persistence of Lee Iacocca as he rescues the Chrysler Corporation from bankruptcy. We applaud the creativity and initiative of Steven Jobs of Apple Computer as he builds a major new corporation on emerging microprocessor technology. These corporate giants are risk takers, dreamers, and innovators, and they embody the distinctive characteristics of the organization whose future they shape. They are strategists. They have the capacity and opportunity to view their organization as a whole, assess the emerging marketplace within which they will operate, and make decisions that will best match their organization's strengths with changing external conditions and opportunities.

Critics of the condition of educational management apparently do not expect organizational leaders like Iacocca and Jobs to emerge from within higher education. Martin (1983, p. 41) expresses the opinion that educational administrators are programmed for routine, operational management: "Consequently, it is absurd to expect them to retrain voluntarily for education leadership. Administrators who attempt such a change would encounter an identity crisis, because the effort would involve repudiation of the style as well as substance of a

G. A. Myran (Ed.). *Strategic Management in the Community College.* New Directions for Community Colleges, no. 44. San Francisco: Jossey-Bass, December 1983.

professional life with which they have been identified and satisfied. They could not swallow the criticism implicit in such a transformation, nor could they find the courage to regroup around new rewards and functions." The opinions of Martin and other critics notwithstanding, an academic management revolution is taking place, and it centers on a change in focus from operational to strategic management. Keller (1982, pp. 3-4) writes: "The academic management revolution contains four major shifts. One is the move from administration to management. Administration, the efficient arrangement of everyday activities from student registration and class schedules to fund raising and appointments, has usually taken the overwhelming proportion of time of the presidents, vice-presidents, and deans. Administrative work is internally focused and temporally myopic in many cases. Next year's budget is often the limit for the future horizon. Administration is vital, important. But, management—the active, entrepreneurial shaping of an organization's or institution's future life—is rapidly emerging as a larger factor in the lives of many academic executives. Unlike administration, management tends to be outwardly focused: scanning the changing markets, the competition, the new conditions and probable directions of science, intellect, and art. It looks three, five, or seven years ahead, watching trends and forecasts like a submarine commander at his periscope."

Community College Management

What does it mean to manage a community college? If this question were addressed to a group of traditional community college managers, they would probably offer such definitions as *to produce results* or *to direct and control.* They would choose synonyms of the verb *manage,* such as *lead, execute, plan, operate, run,* or *guide.* These definitions and synonyms are based on an assumption that the organization has a hierarchical structure in the shape of a pyramid that is run by managers at the top. Adizes (1979) suggests that we would be better advised to think of an hourglass shape than of a pyramid. Such an organizational structure for community college is illustrated in Figure 1.

This hourglass diagram places management in the vortex between the dynamics of the external environment on the one hand and the dynamics of the internal environment on the other. Management occupies a catalytic, integrative leadership role in influencing the future of the college. To play such a role, the community college manager must add to the traditional repertory of skills (producing, directing, and controlling) a battery of future-oriented skills that

Figure 1. Organizational Structure

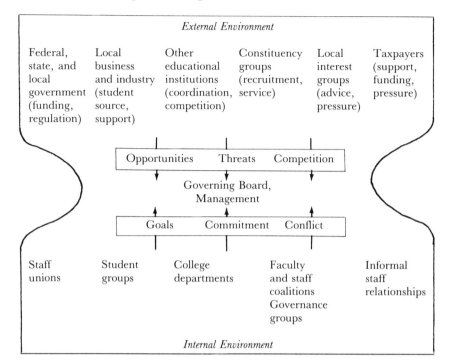

involve building external and internal relationships, assessing future opportunities and threats, and formulating and implementing strategy.

A Definition of Strategic Management

The definition of strategy has broadened over time from one with strictly military connotation (planning and directing large troop movements) to one that encompasses the efforts of persons in any organization to see their enterprise as a whole, to envision the relation between the enterprise and external social, economic, and political forces, and to make decisions that create the best future for the enterprise in a changing and turbulent environment.

Rumelt (1979) states that the basic task of strategy is to frame an uncertain situation into more comprehensible subproblems or tasks that fall within the competence of the organization. Hosmer (1978, p. 2) defines strategy as "a process which includes both the definition of the goals and objectives of an institution and the design of major policies and plans and the organizational structure and systems to achieve those objectives—all in response to changing environmental conditions, institutional resources, and individual motives and values." Hatten (1982, p. 104) describes the purposes of strategic management as follows: "Strategic management provides a framework for organizational analysis which can facilitate managerial decision making. It forces the manager to consider various critical dimensions of the organization and so is likely to improve organizational performance both in its provision of services and its effective use of resources and control of costs." Hatten (1982, p. 102) further describes strategic management as a process that "(1) determines and maintains a viable set of relationships between the organization and its environment, (2) systematizes the evaluation of organizational performance, (3) sets directions for the organization's long-term development, (4) uses major resource allocation programs to pursue the organization's objectives, matching capabilities with the opportunities and threats of the environment, (5) provides guidelines for any appropriate change in the organizational structure required to implement further development, (6) gives diverse participants, from varied and sometimes contentious functional areas, a common experience and concepts on which to base discussions of future development, (7) explicitly matches strategies and situations in an active administrative process, and (8) requires a systematic evaluation of the position of the organization in its environment."

Stiner and Miner (1977) suggest that there are four key overall forces in strategy: key external environmental forces, key internal environmental forces, policy/strategy areas, and key elements determining responses to environmental impacts. Figure 2 represents these strategic forces in the community college setting.

It is clear from these definitions and descriptions that strategic management, adapted to the community college, deals with the fundamental questions that the college must answer if it is to know its social role—or, to express it more directly, what business it is in: What is the clientele to be served? What community educational needs are to be met? What external and internal relationships are to be established and nurtured? How are the college's human, financial, and physical resources to be developed or reallocated? What structure of programs and services should be supported and developed? Should the college grow, stabilize, reduce, or rebuild?

The answers to these fundamental questions become the building blocks for determining institutional strategy. The following definitions of *strategy* and *strategic management* in the community college emphasize the process of seeking answers to these fundamental questions: A strategy is a definite course of action that is adopted by college

Figure 2. Strategic Forces

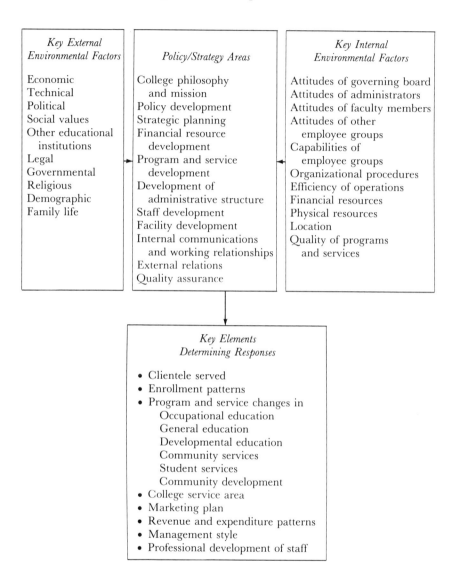

Key External Environmental Factors	*Policy/Strategy Areas*	*Key Internal Environmental Factors*
Economic	College philosophy	Attitudes of governing board
Technical	and mission	Attitudes of administrators
Political	Policy development	Attitudes of faculty members
Social values	Strategic planning	Attitudes of other
Other educational	Financial resource	employee groups
institutions	development	Capabilities of
Legal	Program and service	employee groups
Governmental	development	Organizational procedures
Religious	Development of	Efficiency of operations
Demographic	administrative structure	Financial resources
Family life	Staff development	Physical resources
	Facility development	Location
	Internal communications	Quality of programs
	and working relationships	and services
	External relations	
	Quality assurance	

Key Elements Determining Responses

- Clientele served
- Enrollment patterns
- Program and service changes in
    Occupational education
    General education
    Developmental education
    Community services
    Student services
    Community development
- College service area
- Marketing plan
- Revenue and expenditure patterns
- Management style
- Professional development of staff

leadership in order to shape the character, scope, and direction of the college. Strategic management is a future-creating process that guides and integrates the various strategies and decisions of the college in such a way that the college as a whole is positioned favorably in relation to emerging opportunities and threats in the external environment.

Components of Strategic Management

There are four basic steps in strategic management in the community college: building relationships, assessing goals and trends, forming strategy, and implementing decisions based on the first three steps. Figure 3 illustrates the relationship among these components.

Building relationships in the external and internal environment is the foundation of strategic management. Externally, the working relationships that exist with citizens, employers, legislators, government officials, community leaders, donors, and potential students provide the framework for specific outcomes that will occur as a result of the relationship. The long-term strategy is the creation of the solid network of relationships; the short-term strategy has more immediate goals. Internal relationships with faculty groups, administrators, clerical staff, custodial staff, and unionized groups are designed to release the intelligence and energy of all staff groups in dealing with strategic matters. The strategic element of internal relationships involves the creation and maintenance of a climate of participation and responsibility on the part of all staff groups.

Assessment of external and internal conditions and trends inevitably draws on the data collection and data analysis component of strategic management. External assessment involves the analysis of opportunities and threats and the anticipation of events that may affect the college in the future. Specific assessments can include studies of emerging educational needs of present and potential constituencies; analysis of economic, political, social and demographic trends; and analysis of the strengths and weaknesses of college competition. Assessment of internal conditions can include examination of past and present strategies to understand why they succeeded or failed and of the changes that are needed. It can also involve systematic analysis of the strengths and

Figure 3. Components of Strategic Management

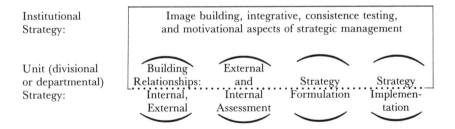

weaknesses of each unit or functional area of the college as that unit or area relates to future potential. It can include assessment of the strengths and weaknesses of management as it relates to future potential and the identification of distinctive or special qualities of the college on which future development can be built.

Strategy formulation takes place at both institutional and unit (divisional and departmental) levels. The image-building, integrative, consistency-testing, and motivational aspects of strategic management tend to be focused at the institutional level, and they are primarily the responsibilities of the chief executive officer (CEO) and other executive officers. The CEO is the central focus of an institutional value system that supports future and externally oriented strategies. Peters (1979, p. 164) states: "In an untidy world where goal setting, option selection, and policy implementation hopelessly fuzz together, the shaping of robust institutional values through a principle of ad hoc opportunism becomes preeminently the mission of the chief executive officer and his most senior colleagues." Cauwenbergh and Cool (1982, p. 246) view top management as having the responsibility for creating a framework for strategic thinking throughout the organization: "Top management has to secure the survival of the company in an increasingly turbulent environment and hence to animate and monitor strategic behavior at lower levels. It should not try to generate well-documented proposals but has to see that a sufficient number of adequate proposals are formulated at lower levels. Top management ought to be a catalyst of strategic thought and activity for lower-level management."

Institutional strategy can include these elements: establishing and keeping current the college's philosophy and mission statement; articulating the desired future image for the college as a whole, which is based on the college's philosophy and mission statement; creating strategic institutional plans that are shaped to the needs of the preferred future image and to the effective use of human and financial resources; analyzing unit strategies to be certain that they are consistent with conditions in the external environment, existing institutional resources, institutional trends, and the existing institutional climate; integrating unit strategies into a mosaic that depicts the needs of strategic plans and the preferred future image; and designing participative structures and incentives that will utilize staff talents and promote staff commitment to the achievement of institutional and unit strategies.

At the unit level, the formulation of strategy focuses on the future of specific divisions or departments. Ideally, these strategies are shaped to the missions and plans of the college as a whole. Unit strategies can include these elements: program and service development, strategies, financial resource development and reallocation strategies, staff development strategies, physical facilities development strategies, and quality assurance strategies. At the unit level there should also be a process that encourages the formulation of institutional strategies that will help to shape a preferred future for both the unit and the college of which is is a part.

Finally, strategy implementation involves the development and implementation of action plans that attend to organizational aspects of the strategy: who will do what and when specific steps will be taken. Implementation should also include the development of a system to monitor progress of strategies and specific decision-making processes and the necessary evaluation and reconceptualization of strategies.

Strategic and Operational Management

Strategic management deals with steering the organization, and operational management deals with keeping it on course. Strategic management creates a framework of relationships, assessments, and strategies within which operational management can take place effectively. The future-oriented, entrepreneurial, creative, long-term nature of strategic management complements the present-oriented, logical, sequential, short-term nature of operational management.

Strategic activities take place in all areas and at all levels of community college functioning. In each functional area, decisions are made that relate to the development of that area that, when brought into harmony with decisions in other functional areas, represent a self-definition of the college's future from the perspective of the decision makers involved. There is therefore a dynamic interaction between policy/strategy decisions made by top management and the governing board and strategic operational decisions made by faculty and staff members at other levels.

Operational activities take place in all areas and at all levels of the community college. Managers at each level meet deadlines, establish and follow rules and regulations, plan and implement specific programs and services, maintain schedules, prepare and implement contracts, develop and manage annual budgets, and supervise and coordinate staff. In general, operational activities take place in increasing proportion from the highest to the lowest management levels; the opposite is true of strategic management. Figure 4 illustrates the importance of communications among management levels. Middle managers (associate deans, directors, and so forth) play a pivotal role, because they tend to experience both the strategic and operational elements of

Figure 4. Strategic and Operational Management
Strategic Management/Policy Development

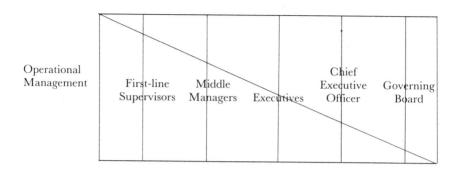

college management; as a result, they can develop insights of great value to executives. Executives must maintain effective communication with those in operational roles to ensure that institutional strategies are informed and influenced by operational concerns and to assist managers at all levels to make decisions that are consistent with institutional strategies.

Adizes (1979, p. 5) asserts that there are four essential management roles. Two are strategically oriented, and two are operationally oriented: "The necessary and sufficient management roles that need to be performed for the long run effective and efficient operations of an organization are: to produce, to administer, to be an entrepreneur, and to integrate." Production and administration are operationally oriented. Production in the community college involves achieving specific results in occupational education, general education, developmental education, community services, student services, and community development. Administration in the community college setting involves activities that ensure that systems work the way in which they are designed to work. Entrepreneurship and integration are strategically oriented. Entrepreneurship in the community college involves the creation of strong relationships with area business and industry, present and potential constituency groups, and other community agencies and groups whose actions or decisions can create opportunities for the college. It involves the identification of possible new or modified modes of service in which the college might respond to changing community needs. Integration in the community college involves the efforts of staff groups to move forward in a chosen direction or to change direction. Integration focuses on group problem solving and on processes that release the creativity, intellect, and talents of all persons involved in a work group.

Building a Management Team

No one person in a community college can simultaneously perform all management roles. In fact, quite often these roles are in conflict. Those who have entrepreneurial roles tend to conflict with those who have administrative roles and who wish to run a tight ship. Those who are oriented toward producing results tend to conflict with those who wish to engage in integrating activities, particularly when the task involves immediate time pressures. Because no one person can carry out all necessary management roles and because each administrator has different strengths and management styles, it is essential to focus on developing a management team. In an effective management team, each member recognizes the particular roles, strengths, and management styles of other team members. Team members learn to rely on the strengths of other team members so that their activities are integrated. Team members also learn that, since the essential management roles are at times in conflict, it is natural and healthy for some conflict to occur. The challenge for the entire team is to deal effectively with conflict rather than to avoid or eliminate it.

Methodology of Strategic Management

Community colleges use a wide variety of methods to carry out strategic management. The most common method involves the periodic development of a written long-range plan, but there are many other methods as well. One college uses strategy position papers—documents that are developed for a specific strategy area and distributed throughout the college for reaction. Another uses strategy sessions called *president's workshops* to bring staff groups together to discuss particular strategic issues. Several colleges have college planning and development committees made up of representatives from various staff groups; these committees are the primary deliberative and advisory bodies on strategic matters. Many colleges have monthly, quarterly, or annual strategy workshops or retreats involving various staff groups. Most chief executive officers have an executive committee that focuses on strategic matters from a management point of view. A few have so-called planning rooms designed for small-group strategic discussions; wall displays portray the changing results of strategic deliberations. Many colleges use breakfast meetings, regularized community visits, and newsletters to establish and maintain external relationships and involve external groups in strategic deliberations. A few colleges form "future of the college" committees made up of citizens and staff members. Other collaborative approaches bring staff union groups and managers together to deal with strategic matters. Generally, nearly all colleges are experimenting with new structures and groups that deliberate on strategic matters.

The Need for Strategic Management

Historically, the entrepreneurial strategically oriented administrator or faculty member in the community college has functioned primarily as an individual, although often he or she has received enthusiastic support from other staff persons. All community colleges have examples of staff members whose individual efforts brought a new student group into the college, created a major new program, or established a significant new relationship in the community. However, only in recent years have conditions both inside and outside the college stimulated systematic approaches to the search for new opportunities, the creation of internal processes to promote future-oriented dialogue, and the integration of the various commitments that have been made to shape the college's future.

Several external and internal conditions have encouraged more cohesive, future-creating processes. First, in a period of financial scarcity, it is no longer feasible to rely on the incremental approach to creating the institutional future. New programs can no longer be added without careful attention to the continued allocation of resources to existing programs. Innovative strategies must involve a form of horizontal growth, where high-priority programs are added, changed, or expanded while lower-priority programs are eliminated or reduced. The period of vertical or incremental growth has probably ended for most community colleges.

A second condition has evolved from the turbulent environment within which community colleges exist. Changes in demographics, the economy, the number and diversification of competitors, sources of revenue, industrial and business technologies, and government policies all create uncertainties about the path ahead. Colleges must orchestrate and manage these varied and often conflicting messages from the external environment. The economic and political events of recent years have served to remind community colleges how dependent their future is on external conditions and trends. While internal forces may determine the ebb and flow of some academic decisions, the economic and political decisions that shape the future of the college are made externally.

A third condition arises from the increasing demands among employee groups to participate in decisions that will determine the future of the college and of their programs. Effective strategic processes integrate dialogue about the future of the various components of the college into a shared image of the future of the college as a whole.

A fourth condition emerges from the need to identify more clearly the scope and mission of the community college. Today, community colleges must identify and build on the areas in which they are distinctive. Colleges should be aware of their comparative advantages over other educational institutions and use this awareness in developing strategy. Every community college must find its niche in the marketplace if it is to avoid confusion among both clientele and staff groups. Regardless of the strategy used, there is an increasing need for focus and clearer institutional identity in the communities served by the college.

Choosing the Community College Future

Naisbitt (1982, p. 252) believes that we are living the "time of the parenthesis," a time of rapid change between the industrial and the information eras: "Although the time between eras is uncertain, it is a great and yeasty time, filled with opportunity. If we can make uncertainty our friend, we can achieve much more than in stable times... in the time of the parenthesis we have extraordinary leverage and influence — individually, professionally, and institutionally — if we can only get a clear sense, a clear conception, a clear vision of the road ahead." If we are to grasp emerging opportunities, Naisbitt suggests, we must develop an ability to anticipate the future. He asserts that, in this period of rapid transition from the industrial to the information era, we must learn to draw lessons from the anticipation of future conditions and trends, just as we have traditionally drawn on lessons from the past.

Community colleges are in the parenthesis between two eras that parallel the transitional nature of society as a whole. The growth era for community colleges is fading, and the vitality era is emerging. The key concern of the next decade will not be whether community colleges can survive but whether they can continue to be vital to the students, communities, and employers that they serve. A vital, anticipatory, active, high-performance approach to creating the future must be found, or colleges will decline into a passive and stultifying repetition of increasingly outmoded services. More than in the past, community college leaders will create the future of their institutions by the choices that they make. And, choose they must. As the pace of technological, economic, political, and social change continues to accelerate, community college leaders must choose among the external and internal stimuli that demand attention and analysis. They must choose between alternative scenarios for the development of the college in response to these stimuli, and they must choose how the limited human, physical, and financial resources of the college should be developed and allocated.

How can community college leaders best make the choices that will determine institutional viability and shape the future of these colleges? How can we make uncertainty our friend? How will we get a clear vision of the college in the future? First, changes in perspective and orientation must take place. We must shift from an operational to a strategic perspective and from a short-term to a long-term perspective. A past-and-present orientation must be replaced by a future orientation.

Second, we must develop and use the entrepreneurial, adaptive, and planning skills of strategic management. Most community college administrators are skilled operational managers. Their career steps and their professional rewards have been based on operational excellence. Clearly, operational management is essential to the smooth functioning of the college. In a stable period, the effective carrying out of operational tasks might even be sufficient to ensure the viability of the college, but it will not be sufficient in a period of social and economic turbulence and change. In such a period, community college managers must be able to steer the college — create and shape its future — as well as to keep it running smoothly.

Third, we must infuse strategic management into the functioning of community colleges. Of course, community colleges engage in strategy making now. Examples of strategies that community colleges adopted and pursued in recent years include capturing a significant share of the area educational television market; promoting growth and excellence in instructional programs serving high technology industries; developing a structure of open-entry, open-exit instructional programs; creating a focus on institutional marketing; developing quality circles and other forms of staff participation; and fostering programs of quality control. Each of these strategies will certainly contribute to shaping the future of community colleges. What is typically missing, however, is a process that integrates the individual strategies into a viable institutional plan. Strategy making that is not integrated into an institutional whole will direct the organization in a confusing, random fashion, and it can easily overload institutional systems. In the past, such shortcomings in strategic management could be tolerated, because growth produced investment revenues for an ever widening circle of strategy making. However, in a period of limited resources and increased public demand for quality and accountability, each strategic decision must be weighed carefully in relation to other strategies and to external and internal realities.

Obviously, an integrated, systematic process for strategy making in community colleges is needed, but developing such a process is never easy. Creating a strategic management process in a community college will be resisted, because it takes time and energy, it requires new skills and insights, and it may expose the shortcomings of present strategies. The development of a strategic management process must begin with an understanding of the commitment, time, and energy required to ensure success. Yet, the development of these processes is taking place in community colleges everywhere. Community colleges are in the midst of a revolution in management style. Managers are learning new ways to weave together the interests and expectations of the community, the governing board, administrators, faculty, students, and other groups in ways that determine the college's distinctive characteristics and contours for the future. Those within community colleges realize that the organizational future does not just happen. Rather, creating the future starts with the key decision makers at all levels, and it is given shape by their will and energy.

References

Adizes, I. *How to Solve the Management Crisis.* San Francisco: Adizes Institute, 1979.

Cauwenbergh, A. V., and Cool, K. "Strategic Management in a New Framework." *Strategic Management Journal,* 1982, *3* (3), 245–264.

Hatten, M. L. "Strategic Management in Not-For-Profit Organization." *Strategic Management Journal,* 1982, *3* (2), 89–104.

Hosmer, L. T. *Academic Strategy.* Ann Arbor: University of Michigan, 1978.

Keller, G. "The New Management Revolution in Higher Education." *AAHE Bulletin,* October 1982, *35,* 3–4.

Martin, W. B. "Education for Character, Career, and Society." *Change,* 1983, *15* (1), 35–42.

Naisbitt, J. *Megatrends.* New York: Warner Books, 1982.

Peters, T. "Leadership: Sad Facts and Silver Lining." *Harvard Business Review,* 1979, *57,* 164–172.

Rumelt, R. P. "Evaluation of Strategy: Theory and Models." In D. E. Schendle and C. W. Hofer (Eds.), *Strategic Management.* Boston: Little, Brown, 1979.

Stiner, G. A., and Miner, J. B. *Management Policy and Strategy.* New York: Macmillan, 1977.

Gunder A. Myran is president of Washtenaw Community College in Ann Arbor, Michigan, and an adjunct professor in the Center for the Study of Higher Education at the University of Michigan.

A comprehensive community college is, to a great extent, the sum of its external relationships, for the totality of these relationships defines the mission, role, and scope of the community college.

Strategic Elements of External Relationships

James F. Gollattscheck

The relationships between a community college and the wide variety of external groups and individuals surrounding it are most often different from similar relationships involving other educational institutions. They are different both in terms of their importance and in their very nature. In community colleges, relationships with many external groups and individuals are as important as any of the college's internal relationships. While other types of educational institutions may depend on external groups and individuals for financial and political support, for public relations and goodwill, and in some cases for a degree of governance, a comprehensive community college is, to a great extent, the sum of its external relationships, for the totality of these relationships defines the mission, role, and scope of the community college.

More than any other activity, the community college's relationships with external groups and individuals determine how the community perceives the college. This in turn determines the ways in which the community uses the services of the college and the extent to which the college is allowed to become involved in meeting the needs of the community. Regardless of its stated mission, a community college can be

G. A. Myran (Ed.). *Strategic Management in the Community College.* New Directions for Community Colleges, no. 44. San Francisco: Jossey-Bass, December 1983.

nothing more than the community thinks it is. A college can state in its publications that it is a comprehensive community-based community college, yet if the people whom it serves look on it as a liberal arts institution offering only a transfer degree, then for all practical purposes that is what it is.

For the college that wishes to be a comprehensive community-based institution, appropriate and effective external relationships are essential. The quality of these relationships will determine the college's success in developing and delivering community-based programs. In a recent study of community-based education in American community colleges, McGuire (1982, p. 10) defined community-based education as follows: "Community-based education is a learner-centered philosophy of lifelong learning which is committed to the continuous renewal of the community and all of its citizens. It is based on an institutional value system which 1, places the learning needs of the student above the teaching needs of the educational institution; 2, recognizes a special relationship between the institution and the community, in which the institution determines its missions, goals, and objectives through interaction with the community; and, 3, requires that the institution's programs and services focus on those competencies, both knowledges and skills, that are essential for the learner to be an effective, productive citizen in the community." It is easy to see how vital the relationships between the college and external groups and individuals in the community are to the achievement of this mission.

Finally, the quality of some of these relationships will determine the support that the college receives from its community and state. For colleges with only local funding, it is obvious that the college cannot succeed in fulfilling any of its missions without a base of understanding and support from the local community to whom local elected officials report and respond. Colleges with only state-level support or a combination of state and local support have an even more complex set of relationships with which to deal. State elected officials must be convinced by local citizens of the need for adequate funding for college programs.

A community college exists in the context of a wide variety of relationships with individuals and groups in its surrounding community, region, and state. As a college concerned with meeting the needs of people, it must be concerned with the quality of the relationships that it has developed and that it is developing with such groups and individuals. Its very existence as a community college is dependent to a great extent on its success in developing and maintaining good external relationships.

Strategic Management of External Relationships

The strategic management of external relationships is frequently overlooked even by institutions most involved in strategic management. The management of such resources as dollars, personnel, and facilities and the management of the college's mission-related activities, such as recruitment, curriculum, and instructional strategy, have most often been the target of strategic management and planning. Throughout this volume, strategic management is looked on as the elements of management that shape the future of the college. External relationships have seldom been looked at for what they actually are — one of the major factors that shapes the future of the college either directly and deliberately through planning and management or indirectly and haphazardly through neglect.

While the management of external relationships is critical for all the reasons just discussed, there are two other very important reasons why external relationships should be considered in any program of strategic management. First, since the college exists not in a vacuum but in a dynamic environment all aspects of which are continuously interacting, it is impossible to conduct an effective program of strategic management in other areas without an in-depth knowledge of the strategic elements of the college's external relationships. For example, it would be foolish to become involved in a study of new delivery systems that might allow the college to reach new clientele in the future if those responsible for such plans do not understand the past, present, and potential relationships between the college and individuals and groups representing or involved with that particular clientele.

Second, the development of appropriate and effective external relationships is fundamental to the achievement of almost all other missions, goals, and objectives of the community college. For example, even the most traditional of missions — that of offering a transfer degree to students who wish to pursue a four-year college degree — cannot be truly effective if the college has not established good relationships with secondary schools in its service area and with the colleges and universities to which its students may want to transfer. Such missions as providing occupational programs leading to employment in local business and industry or providing community services and programs of continuing education are even more obviously based on an understanding of the dynamics of the total community.

Scope of External Relationships

The college that wishes to include the elements of external relationships in its strategic management system must include the total scope of such relationships. The college must examine the spectrum of external groups and individuals with whom it is possible to establish relationships and the various types of relationships possible.

With Whom Should the Community College Establish External Relationships? The answer to this question is rather simple: The community college should establish relationships with any and all groups and individuals in its community, region, and state who can help the institution to achieve its stated missions. The broader and more comprehensive its missions are, the wider the range of groups and individuals with whom the college can and should develop appropriate and effective relationships. The comprehensive community-based institution will find it useful to have good working relationships with individuals and groups throughout its community. The institution must examine its missions and goals, then look to the surrounding community, region, and state to determine those individuals and groups with whom it should have some type of relationship in order to achieve its missions.

Of course, there are many elements in a community that affect and ultimately determine the total quality of the community and therefore of the community college. There are man-made facilities, such as parks, buildings, and roads, and there are environmental factors, such as climate and natural resources. Most important, however, for the future both of the community and of the college are the elements composed of people, because only people are capable of thoughtful concern for development, and only people can establish working relationships. While the ways of classifying the strategic human elements of communities are endless, Gollattscheck (1981) identified and defined six broad categories that include most groups and individuals whom a community college should consider in planning for strategic management of external relationships: associations, institutions, agencies, businesses, constituencies, and individual effecters.

Associations are groups of persons acting together for a particular purpose. Membership is generally voluntary, and except for a few paid professionals and other staff in some large associations, most participants receive no monetary compensation, although dues are frequently charged to operate the organization. Most clubs, societies, and leagues fall into this category. Of all the elements in a community, associations are probably the most numerous and the most varied in terms of size, complexity, purpose, and general effectiveness.

Institutions are establishments created for the purpose of some objective, generally one of public good, such as education, religion, health, or charity. Churches, schools, colleges, asylums, hospitals, libraries, museums, and some theaters are institutions. Institutions are usually more formally structured than associations, frequently involving legal incorporation. They are more likely to own or lease buildings and other facilities for their own and public use. There are generally more paid staff members performing services, and the public may be involved through memberships, for which a fee is charged or a contribution is expected, or through payment for services. Institutions can be tax-supported or independent, but they are usually nonprofit.

Agencies are working arms of federal, state, or local government, such as courts, boards, commissions, law enforcement and welfare units, parks and recreation departments, and planning councils, to name but a few. Agencies are tax-supported, but they can charge fees. They are chartered in law or regulation. The can be service or control-oriented.

Businesses operate for profit, selling goods, services, or both. They involve the people of the community either as employees or as customers.

Constituencies are groups of individuals with one or more common characteristics, such as need, interest, problem, age, handicap, nationality, or sex. Constituencies may or may not be organized in any manner, although many—the elderly and the handicapped for example—are forming associations to put organized pressure on the community and government to provide services. Constituencies are a convenient way of inventorying the public. However, it must be remembered that many individuals can be included in several constituency groups, while others do not fit readily into any of the more frequently identified constituencies. It must also be remembered that the more organized and vocal a constituency is, the more likely it is to be recognized. Nevertheless, its vocal ability reveals nothing significant about its size, the seriousness of its needs, or its capabilities as a community resource.

Individual effecters are persons who, although they function within or from the base of an organization or constituency, must be singled out as an element of the community because of the effect that their opinions, words, actions, and support have in and on the community beyond any one organization or constituency. These persons can gain such positions for a variety of reasons, such as wealth, social position, effectiveness as a leader, political power, business influence, or personality. Individual effecters are not always obvious. Careful scrutiny of the powers at work in a community can reveal that, while many people operate on the surface with much attention, some of the people who are extremely effective are seldom or never publicly visible.

It must be remembered that any such categorization of the human elements of a community is artifical and therefore difficult to apply in real situations. Lines between categories are sometimes difficult to distinguish. Is a proprietary school a business or an institution? Is a public tax-supported college an institution or an arm of government and therefore an agency? Is a private hospital an institution or a business? Division into categories is for purposes of discussion, analysis, and planning; it need not be rigid.

It is also important to remember that one type of organization can create an organization of a different type to perform a function that it cannot because of constraints and limitations of its particular structure. For example, a museum (an institution) can create a "friends of the museum" group (an association) in order to avoid the limitations inherent in a legally incorporated institution or to make it easier to involve volunteers. A corporation (a business) can form a foundation (an association or an institution) in order to gain the best advantages from corporate philanthropy. A college (an institution) can create a business to conduct some profit-making enterprise. If such spin-offs are ignored, an important group with whom the college should establish strategic relationships may be overlooked.

What Types of Strategic Relationships Are Possible? The mission of the college will determine to a great extent the types of external relationships that it should develop. The college with a somewhat narrow mission may find that it needs only advisory and supportive relationships. In contrast, the comprehensive community-based institution may find that it needs a wide range of types of external relationships reflective of its desire to cooperate with the total community in its effort to help the community renew itself. These relationships must, of course, go far beyond support and information-supplying arrangements. They will be developed to help the college carry out a mission, to help the external group to achieve one or more of its purposes, or both. These relationships can require mutual involvement in planning, conducting, and evaluating learning experiences. They can be formal, informal, simple, complex, unilateral, multilateral, temporary, long-term, or whatever arrangement is appropriate to the particular situation.

Relationships between a community college and groups and individuals in the community can range from casual awareness to total involvement. Ultimately, the type of relationship developed depends on what is perceived as possible and desirable by the college and by the community organization. Obviously, both the college and groups and individuals in the community must perceive a mutuality of interests and benefits for any relationship to develop and endure. For purposes of analysis, one can identify five distinct types of relationships. It must be remembered, however, that the continuing relationship between the college and an organization is likely to involve several different modes of operation, with the relationship changing from one mode to another as situations and needs dictate (Gollattscheck and others, 1976).

The most elementary relationship between a college and groups and individuals in the community is awareness. Awareness can be mutual or one-directional. If support—in terms of policy making, financial support, and influence—is the primary goal of the relationship, then awareness may be completely satisfactory. Levels of awareness can range from casual knowledge of the existence of the entity to total understanding. Awareness requires no participation in activities and does not require real mutuality of interests between the college and the group or organization. The purpose of many public relations programs is to develop some level of awareness of the college, its programs, and its needs among groups and individuals in the community.

An advisory relationship is the most common participatory arrangement between community colleges and groups and individuals in the community. The use of community advisory committees by a college is quite common. However, a community-based college will find itself and its people used more and more in an advisory capacity by various elements in the community as its interest in the community and its potential for assistance become more widely known. Advisory relationships can be temporary for a project of short duration or long-range for a continuing college program. Because the advisory arrangement is one of the simplest and most common types of external relationships that a college can have with groups and individuals in the community, its great value should not be underrated. The college that has developed a broad range of types of relationships with strategic elements in the community will still rely heavily on the use of organizations and agencies in advisory capacities.

Direct assistance is the provision of services, facilities, expertise, or other resources. Like advisory assistance, direct assistance can pass from the college to the community or vice versa. For example, the college can develop and offer a course at the request of an association, or an institution in the community can provide facilities for the college. The duration of these arrangements will be determined by the nature of the project. Direct assistance relationships are more formal than advisory relationships, and they should be spelled out in contracts if funds, personnel, or similar resources are involved. Colleges frequently provide direct assistance to associations or institutions who wish to serve particular constituencies but who do not have the resources or expertise to provide the service. Community colleges frequently request direct assistance from an existing community association, institution, or agency when instituting a program to provide a service within the college would result in needless duplication, overlapping of programs, or waste of resources.

When the college and an element of the community work together in a truly cooperative educational enterprise, the relationship is a joint venture. Joint venture arrangements are more formal than advisory relationships, and the contract should spell out the duties and obligations of each party to prevent misunderstanding as the project develops. In an ideal joint venture, each party's strengths will complement the other party's weaknesses. For example, a community college and a community association decided to establish a parent education program and a cooperative daycare center. This joint venture involved the provision of educational expertise and other services by the college and funding and other considerations by the association. The two institutions signed an agreement whereby the association supported the project with a grant of money and 5,000 volunteer hours annually, while the community college provided staffing, facilities, and support services for the project.

The other end of the continuum that begins with casual awareness and covers the range of possible relationships between community colleges and community organizations is the merger. In a merger, a college and an organization, perceiving themselves to have common interests with respect to a particular targeted constituency or activity, contract to pool their resources in a long-term cooperative enterprise in which each bears specified responsibilities and shares in the benefits. Mergers are extremely formal and must be spelled out in legal contracts. A merger does not necessarily require that either party to the merger give up its identity. For example, a local community association established to broker continuing education for women in the community merged with a local community college. It became the college's Center for Continuing Education for Women while maintaining its independent community identity as the Council for Continuing Education for Women in the area. The importance of retaining individual identities should not be overlooked. A community organization can maintain contacts in the community that a public body, such as a community college, frequently cannot. The community organization may also find it easier to recruit volunteers and get publicity than the institution.

The types of arrangements that can evolve between a college and external groups and individuals are limited only by the needs of the institution to work with various elements of its community to achieve its missions; the readiness and willingness of the institution and its people to bring outside elements of the community into its planning, operation, and evaluation functions not only as supporters and information suppliers, but also as partners; creativeness of the institution in developing arrangements that may be very new to its own members and to the groups and individuals that it touches in the community.

Developing Effective and Appropriate External Relationships

As in any process of management, strategic or operational, activities relate to planning, implementation, and evaluation.

Planning for Strategic Management of External Relationships. Planning activities must begin with the establishment of goals and objectives for the process. These goals and objectives must grow out of and further the missions, goals, and objectives of the community college. Those that do not should be discarded, unless it is decided in the planning process that overall institutional missions, goals, and objectives should be modified or expanded.

One approach is to review the existing missions, goals, and objectives of the college, specifying the implications for strategic management of external relationships of each specific mission, goal, and objective. For example, if one of the college's goals is to provide opportunities allowing disabled persons in the community to further their education and become more productive citizens, then a goal relating to strategic management of external relationships will be to identify and develop appropriate and effective relationships with all organizations and individuals in the community who represent, provide services to, and have knowledge of handicapped persons in the community. Depending upon the modus operandi of the college, the purpose of this goal can be to gather information, to develop two-way communication, or to establish appropriate joint ventures.

Another appropriate planning activity is to assess the external environment of the college to determine the groups and individuals in the community with which relationships already exist and the groups and individuals with which relationships should be established. If the college has an ongoing program of community analysis, such information is already available. Since needs assessments, which focus on needs and ignore strengths and resources in the community, are more common than community analyses, which gather information about and develop descriptions of the total community's needs and resources, it is a safe assumption that these data have not been gathered in most institutions.

Using some categorization of strategic elements of the community, such as the one outlined earlier in this chapter, those responsible for planning should ask, What associations exist in the community with whom the college has some type of relationship? What are the natures of these relationships? What associations exist in the community with whom the college should develop some type of relationship in order to achieve its missions, goals, and objectives? What should be the nature of these relationships? The same questions should be asked for institutions, agencies, businesses, constituencies, and individuals. The outcome of such a process would be a profile of the community's organizational structure as it exists and as it relates to the college. The profile should help college planning staff begin to develop plans for strategic management of external relationships by showing clearly where the college has developed relationships and where gaps exist. For example, the study could show that three associations, one agency, and one institution exist to serve or represent the elderly population. The study could also show that one individual in the community is recognized as the primary representative of elderly citizens in the area. It could be further determined that the college has a working relationship with one association and an awareness of the other association and the individual but that it is somewhat doubtful whether the other association and the individual are aware of the college.

The third planning activity is to develop plans of action. Using the goals and objectives previously developed and the information gathered about the community, plans of action leading to the achievement of specific objectives can be written. Plans of action must not be vague or general if they are to be effective. Exact responsibilities must be assigned to a group or an individual, the results expected must be detailed, and time limits must be established. Using the example given in the preceding paragraph, it may be determined that the college should attempt to develop two-way advisory relationships with all the elements of the community related to the elderly population. This assignment may be given to an individual or to a committee. The expected results may be that, by a specified date, a personal contact will have been made with each of the elements, an invitation will have been extended for an appropriate person to serve on a college advisory committee, and arrangements will have been made for the college to advise the group or individual of the services and activities at the college of interest to them. Similarly, a plan of action could be developed that called for establishment of a joint venture relationship with one of the associations serving the elderly population.

Since most complex external relationships require mutual awareness, trust, and experience, they tend to evolve from less complex relationships. For this reason, it is probably wise for the college interested in developing joint ventures or mergers to begin with awareness and advisory types of relationships in order to allow organizations and individuals to come to know the college better.

The fourth planning activity is that of developing plans for evaluation. Built into each objective and each plan of action should be specific results and dates when expected results should be achieved. Auditing the results of objectives and plans of action is one way of evaluating progress of strategic management of external relationships. Another is periodic assessment of the achievement of the missions and goals of the process. These periodic audits should be included in the initial plans, and responsibility for them should be assigned to appropriate persons or groups.

Implementing Strategic Management of External Relationships. Involving the college in strategic management of its external relationships, including the development of new or more appropriate external relationships, will in most cases require change on the part of both the people of the college and individuals and groups in the community. For beginning such a process, leaders of the college will do well to analyze carefully what is involved in such change, to take careful steps to ensure readiness for change, and to look at all possible strategies. Myran (1983) has identified six general phases involved in bringing about a successful strategic change: building relationships with groups to be involved, diagnosing the need for change, analyzing support and resistance patterns, placing the change process within the college's priority structure, selecting the change strategy, and operationalizing the strategy.

These six phases must be considered as a college begins to implement strategic management of external resources. The process of building relationships with groups must include the identification of and gathering of information about all groups and individuals to be involved. Many of these data concerning external groups and individuals will have been collected in the planning process described earlier. Those responsible for planning and implementation must remember, however, that it is equally important to identify and study groups and individuals inside the college who must be involved in the strategic management of external relationships. This information will be essential in the third phase, where support and resistance patterns are analyzed.

To build sound working arrangements, the college will need at least the following information about external groups and individuals (Gollattscheck and others, 1976, pp. 57–58):

1. What are the objectives of the organization and the order of priority of these objectives? Are there hidden or tacit objectives as distinct from manifest or stated objectives? Are the objectives of the organization consistent with present commitment of resources?
2. What is the nature of the constituency of the organization? Does serving the target constituency fall within the purview or mission of the college? Can the college respond effectively to the needs of this constituency?
3. How effective is the organization? How effective has the organization been in meeting its objectives in the past? Do the members of the organization support the leaders and the objectives? What are the problems of the organization which limit effectiveness?
4. What are the resources of the organization? What are the physical and human resources of the organization in terms of personnel, time, energy, expertise, facilities, and money? Has the organization used its resources efficiently and effectively in the past? Is the organization willing to commit resources to cooperative endeavors with the college?
5. Who are the leaders of the organization? Who are the most influential and powerful people involved in the organization, and what is their style of leadership? How responsive and responsible are the leaders to the members, and how committed are they to the stated goals and objectives of the organization? How are decisions made? What are the attitudes of the leaders about sharing resources, benefits, and, most of all, the credit or prestige from a joint venture?
6. How effective is communication within the organization and between the organization and its constituency? What are the internal and external channels of communication? Are channels of communication provided for feedback from the constituency?

Those responsible for planning and implementation will need certain information about internal groups and individuals involved in strategic management of external resources: First, who are these individuals? What are their stated responsibilities and authorities? How effective are they as leaders? Which constituencies and groups within the college are under their formal jurisdiction or under their informal influence? Second, are they willing to share in joint planning with community groups and individuals in the strategic management of external resources? Are they willing to share in the leadership function and the decision-making function? Third, are they willing to share responsibilities with external groups and individuals? Fourth, are they willing to share credit for successes with groups outside the college? This study of internal and external groups should point out areas where groups and individuals are ready to establish effective relationships. Where gaps in readiness appear, it will be necessary to develop appropriate incentives and create better understandings of the benefits of cooperation.

Diagnosing the need for change is the step that analyzes college missions, goals, and objectives in view of the college's relationships with external groups and individuals. Needs for developing new relationships or for modifying existing relationships in order for the college to achieve its missions, goals, and objectives more effectively should be identified. These needs should be stated clearly in terms meaningful to groups and individuals both inside and outside the college. This step is accomplished only when all those who are involved understand and accept the need for change and appear willing to work to accomplish it.

Any change in the management or operation of an institution as complex as a college is bound to create areas of support and areas of resistance. Those responsible for the implementation of change must learn who supports it and who resists it and why. Only then can they begin to work to bolster support and attempt to minimize resistance. The process of force field analysis developed by Lewin (1947) may be helpful at this point. In force field analysis, leaders identify the restraining forces and the driving forces in a given situation and attempt to determine the relative strength of each in order to begin to amplify positive driving forces and minimize negative restraining forces.

Placing the identified area of change in the college's existing priority structure is a process of deciding how important the change is; how soon, if ever, it will be implemented; and how much of the college's material and human resources will be committed to it. In a sense, this process is the reality test. Many changes sound important, even necessary, in isolation, but when looked at in the context of total college operations they begin to diminish in importance. It is critical for as many as possible of the groups and individuals who will be involved in implementing the change to be a part of this process of prioritization. Those who give an area of change a high priority are apt to be willing to work to accomplish it and support it.

Selecting appropriate strategies to accomplish desired changes in external relationships is essential to the successful management of such relationships. Unlike internal changes in the institution, changes in external relationships involve many elements outside the college, and strategies must be appropriate and effective not only to college personnel but to the myriad of individuals and groups in the community. Many of these elements may not be as motivated as those inside the college, they may not be accustomed to change, and they may not view the college in the same way as those inside. For these reasons, it is critical for those responsible to know and understand external groups and individuals well enough to select attractive, nonthreatening strategies for implementing desired changes. It must not be assumed that a strategy that works for one group will work for another or that the same strategy will work at all times with the same group. Because a college may be threatening to small groups, who fear that they will be swallowed up by a larger institution, a degree of trust must be developed. Moreover, the college must be reasonably certain that a strategy will work before implementing it. Every successful cooperative endeavor will make it easier to establish a relationship with other organizations.

The final step of implementation is to operationalize the strategy agreed upon. If those inside the college and those outside the college have been involved in planning and in the opening steps of implementation, this final step should flow smoothly. Those responsible will need to evaluate implementation continuously in order to determine whether activities are proceeding on schedule, whether the schedule is practical, and whether those involved are proceeding as planned. If problems arise, plans must be modified immediately so that implementation can be as successful as possible.

Evaluating Strategic Management of External Relationships. The college must remain at all times involved in short-range evaluation and long-range evaluation of its management of external relationships. Short-range evaluation must be continuous so that ineffective strategies can be modified and minor problems can be solved quickly before serious difficulties develop. Short-range evaluation need not always be formal in the sense that written reports and hearings are required. It can be a built-in checkpoint to determine progress toward a deadline, accomplishment of a step in the plan of action, or satisfactory achievement of a specific goal or subgoal. Only if the short-range evaluation reveals difficulties need action be taken.

Long-range evaluation should also be built into the planning process and conducted periodically as part of implementation and at the end of a specific project or goal. These evaluations are more formal, and they should result in written reports. Long-range evaluations can deal rather narrowly with the study of the outcomes of a specific project, such as a joint venture with a community association, or they can deal widely with the overall success of the college in working with its community, such as a study of community impact (Alfred, 1982).

As in all management, the evaluation of strategic management of external relationships loops back into the planning process as outcomes of one project modify plans for another or as the evaluation of one step or activity causes changes in plans for further steps. It is particularly important in the management of external relationships for all parties involved, both inside and outside the college, to be actively involved in planning, conducting, and interpreting the results of evaluations. Only in that way can community participants understand and accept changes or modifications in plans and agreements.

Summary

Strategic management of the community college's external relationships is as essential as strategic management of any other area. External relationships between the community college and groups and individuals in its community define its present and shape its future. Strategic management of such relationships brings them into the planning, implementing, and evaluating processes of the institution and ensures that these important relationships develop along lines consistent with the institution's mission and goals, not haphazardly through neglect. Strategic management of external relationships requires the college to know the community extremely well and to be able to use that knowledge to develop relationships in which the strengths and weaknesses of the college and various community groups complement one another. Since the missions of most community colleges include improvement of the community through college-community interaction, college involvement in solving community problems, and service to groups and individuals in the community, it is only through effective and appropriate relationships with such groups and individuals that the community college can achieve its missions.

References

Alfred, R. L. (Ed.). *Institutional Impacts on Campus, Community, and Business Constituencies.* New Directions for Community Colleges, no. 38. San Francisco: Jossey-Bass, 1982.

Gollattscheck, J. F. "Improving the Health of the Body Politic." In *A Look to Future Years: Projects Regarding the Scope and Process of Community Education.* Washington, D.C.: American Association of Community and Junior Colleges, 1981.

Gollattscheck, J. F., Harlacher, E. L., Roberts, E., and Wygal, B. R. *College Leadership for Community Renewal: Beyond Community-Based Education.* San Francisco: Jossey-Bass, 1976.

36

Lewin, K. "Frontiers in Group Dynamics: Concept, Method, and Reality in Social Science; Social Equalibria and Change." *Human Relations,* 1947, *1,* 5–41.

McGuire, K. B. "The State of the Art in Community-Based Education in the American Community College." Unpublished doctoral disseration, Pepperdine University, 1982.

Myran, G. A. "Strategic Management of Community Services in the Community College." *Catalyst,* 1983, *13* (1), 12–14.

James F. Gollattscheck is president of Valencia Community College in Orlando, Florida.

*Shared governance is not a panacea that instantly can solve
every problem that an organization faces. It works only if
there is total commitment to a trusting, caring, and
cooperative relationship among staff groups.*

The Strategy of Internal Communications and Working Relationships

Dennis W. Bila

The campus community consists of many groups, including trustees,
administration, faculty, support personnel, clerical staff, custodial
staff, maintenance staff, and students. Several of these groups can be
represented by unions, whose main concern is to promote their members' self-interest. It seems an enormous task for management to establish effective communication links and a meaningful working relationship with every group. The two groups most directly involved in the
governance of the institution are management and faculty. They also
have the most in common. Administrators were once faculty, and
many faculty aspire to management roles. One day, the relationship
between a faculty member and administrator may be adversarial, and
the next day, it may be collegial. This chapter will examine the
management-faculty alliance. If an effective model can be developed, it
may be possible to apply it to the rest of the campus community.

An administrator questioning the effectiveness of campus communications might ask, Do faculty receive frequent newsletters? Is the
committee structure in place? How many grievances did we process

G. A. Myran (Ed.). *Strategic Management in the Community College.* New Directions
for Community Colleges, no. 44. San Francisco: Jossey-Bass, December 1983.

last year? Does anyone know of or care about the college mission? While these concerns are important, and they must at some point be addressed, they are primarily structural problems and do not form the basis for effective communications or working relationships.

The management-faculty relationship must be based on complete trust, which will be difficult to achieve at institutions facing retrenchment, where rumors concerning whose program or job is next to be cut will abound. Institutions with a history of solving conflict through the grievance procedure or at the bargaining table will also face difficulties in building trust. The second major aspect of an effective management-faculty relationship is involvement. Management must willingly involve faculty in governance of the institution. Mayhew (1979) feels that faculty advice should be available on all matters involving the institution. He further suggests that one of the first things that an institution in trouble needs to do is to create an effective and formal faculty structure.

The effectiveness of working relationships is then based on a mutual commitment to the building of trust and involvement. Conditions affecting higher education are changing rapidly, and the need for a more cooperative attitude between the faculty and administration should be apparent. Mayhew (1979, p. 8) sounds a dire warning when he states: "It seems inevitable that some institutions will die during the 1980s and 1990s because of finite resources and finite populations of potential students."

The postwar years were rapid growth years for higher education. The Carnegie Council on Higher Education (1980) states that, within the last two decades, enrollments in higher education virtually tripled. During such expansion, cooperative relationships were less important. A crisis one day seems less so the next as new management, faculty, and unions find their niche in an ever-growing institution and expanding economic pie. However, the expansion is clearly over, and for many colleges retrenchment has already begun. The Carnegie Council argues that survival is now the theme for most colleges. Virtually all 3,000 institutions of higher education in the United States are likely to feel a demographic and economic pinch for the next two decades.

Given that the working relationship between management and faculty is important to the operation of the institution, I will first examine why existing structures impede that relationship. Then, I will present a structure that allows a more cooperative attitude to be developed.

Existing Administrative-Faculty Structures

Administrative structures in community colleges and in higher education in general are so similar that they might all have been designed from the same management manual (Minzey, 1982). They represent a top-down management style that places an elected governing board at the top, followed by an appointed president, vice-presidents, deans and associate deans, directors and coordinators, and department heads. If there is any deviation in this structure, it is apt to arise at the department-head level. Department heads are variously categorized as strictly administration, strictly faculty, or some combination of the two.

Johnstone (1981) describes five different kinds of representative faculty groups: faculty senate with no bargaining unit, faculty senate and a bargaining unit as equal partners, faculty senate as a subunit of the bargaining unit, faculty senate in a superordinate role to the bargaining unit, and bargaining unit with no faculty senate.

While the faculty senate with no bargaining unit option represents the greater number of higher education faculty, Hankin (1976) reports that fully 30 percent of the community colleges are organized and bargain collectively. In the larger industrial states, the figure is closer to 95 percent. Kelley and Rodriquez (1977) predict that, on the basis of past and present trends, 85 percent to 90 percent of U.S. public postsecondary institutions will be represented by collective bargaining within the next decade. Regardless of one's philosophical feelings concerning unions on campus, they are a force to be dealt with, especially if effective management-faculty relationships are to be fostered.

Faculty Senate

The problems of the decades ahead will require decisive action by faculty groups, and the sheer size of most faculty senates makes decisiveness impossible. Mayhew (1979) describes two situations where declining enrollments made it necessary to reduce faculty. At the first institution, the president made a difficult decision and notified a number of faculty of termination. Notices were actually sent, although the president hoped that some could be rescinded if financing improved. This seemingly arbitrary action by central administration precipitated a crisis that led directly to the formation of a faculty union and indirectly to the termination of the president's appointment. The second president, facing similar conditions, notified the full faculty of the crisis and asked the senate to develop guidelines for terminating faculty and to make recommendations. Six months after the charge was given, the faculty was still unable to come to grips with a problem whose resolution was so painful. Both presidents made classic errors. The first failed to involve and share responsibility with faculty leadership in such a crucial action. The second president sought involvement from such a large group that action was all but impossible. Faculty representatives are the best judge of proper faculty participation on critical issues.

The main function of a faculty senate is to be an advisory agent on academic matters. Douglas (1980) finds that academic senates are not involved in decision making regarding economic issues and working conditions. However, it is in precisely these areas that faculty need and desire to participate actively, especially in a period of retrenchment. Management may also wish to share with faculty some of the responsibility for difficult decisions in these areas.

Faculty senates are lacking in other important areas as well. Lieberman (1969) observes that senates, especially in state and community colleges, are not likely to have negotiating, actuarial, accounting, and legal expertise needed for effective representation. Senates also lack funding necessary for independent action. Finally, they are not affiliated with state or national organizations that in an alliance with administration, could work for the welfare of the institution by lobbying for increased funding from local, state, and national sources. The effectiveness of faculty senates is succinctly summarized by Kemerer and Baldridge (1981, p. 262): "Senates have been notoriously ineffective at many campuses, particularly those where administrators have long run the show."

Faculty Senate and Separate Bargaining Unit

Julius (1977), among other researchers, reports that faculty senates and bargaining units survive quite well together. However, the groups often have difficulty deciding whether an issue is academic — to be discussed by the senate — or economic — best disposed by the union. Issues often are deliberated separately with different recommendations made to management — hardly a welcome event. For example, Johnstone (1981) states that, at Central Michigan University (CMU), any action is acceptable as long as it is acceptable to the faculty senate, the faculty union, and the administration. A change in the tenure policy at CMU recently was discussed by the senate for more than a year. The recommended change now rests with the union. The union leadership will study the proposed change, and, if they so desire, they will negotiate with management — providing, of course, that management is interested. Such a system of separate deliberations is unacceptable when promptness is necessary.

Lack of sufficient faculty leadership necessary for the proper functioning of two separate groups is also a growing problem, especially at smaller institutions. As members age and problems mount, increasing numbers of faculty are unwilling to accept leadership roles in either union or senate. New faculty, a potential source of leadership, are virtually nonexistent.

Bargaining Unit Only

If the relationship between faculty and management is particularly adversarial, then the union may be unable or unwilling to form a more cooperative working relationship. Kemerer and Baldridge (1981, p. 263) note that "many unions hardly want to become involved directly in reaching painful decisions, much preferring to this to someone else while they retain a veto through the grievance process."

Some of the major criticisms of senates do not apply to faculty unions. The union leadership has expertise and experience in major issues raised by retrenchment, such as wages, benefits, working conditions, and job security. These issues form the heart of the union experience. Further, the leadership can obtain advice and legal asistance from state and national affiliates. While some administrators may not feel especially enlightened by these facts, such outside faculty assistance may prove valuable when retrenchment issues are to be faced. There are two faculty types, however, that management should avoid when decisions have to be made: people who propose to speak for the faculty and do not, and people who do not know what they are doing. When management and faculty confront critical issues together, each member should be experienced in the art of negotiations and have an understanding of the subtleties of compromise. Also, the union leadership has experience in selling difficult situations to the faculty. In all likelihood, it will be a necessary function in the time ahead.

Baldridge and others (1981) report that nearly 40 percent of the community colleges have the union as the sole organized faculty group. This situation raises the question as to who speaks for faculty on nonbargaining concerns. Traditionally, unions have avoided academic issues. Administration has attempted to solve the problem in part by establishing an elaborate committee structure. Also, department heads are used as faculty representatives in discussing nonunion issues. However, the committee structure lacks coordinated faculty leadership, and it is likely to be unrepresentative of the entire group. Also, it usually is incapable of acting decisively on critical matters. More important, it makes little sense for the administration to appoint committee members and department heads, then proclaim that they are faculty representatives. Faculty members generally would prefer to elect their own representatives on all governance issues. Garbarino (1975) suggests that the solution may be to integrate union and senate functions, with senate-style collegiality surviving in important areas.

It is not the purpose of this discussion to imply that faculties need to organize in order to establish effective management-faculty relationships. In fact, unions may intensify the adversarial attitude that exists. However, when the union is the sole representative faculty group, it is there that faculty leadership on all governance issues is likely to be found. Johnstone (1981, p. 178) discusses the problem that faculty and management face in determining who should speak for faculty in academic areas: "The situation suggests the need for a new model, but none has yet been developed to obviate the academic and bargaining schizophrenia that both parties to the collective bargaining process in higher education must experience and live with." A model is needed that preserves the basic structure and integrity of current campus groups. It must also encourage the development of a more cooperative faculty-management relationship.

Quality Circles: Industrial Model

Many academics, especially those bewildered by management by objectives, zero defects, and other scientific management methods, immediately question the worthiness of any program or idea with its roots outside higher education. Nonetheless, if a more cooperative management-labor attitude in industry is possible where the adversarial relationship is intense, we in higher education should be able to profit from the experience in that area. The rapid growth of U.S. industry in postwar years has been followed by a decade of decline. In this, it is not unlike U.S. higher education. A number of factors have contributed to this decline. One key factor was the absence of a cooperative management-labor attitude. Industry has responded in part by implementing quality circles programs.

The quality circles concept is considered by many to be a recent import from Japan. However, the idea actually began with Deming and Juran, both U.S. quality control engineers who went to Japan after World War II to help rebuild its industry. Ishikawa is credited with implementation of the circles model in Japan. The Japanese adapted well to changing conditions with this new management-labor model, and there are now more than a million quality circles in Japan involving more than 11 million people.

As defined by Cleary and others (1982), quality circles represent a process in which workers become more involved in the goals of the organization. The basic assumption is that employees know what their problems are and that they will cooperate in solving them if they are allowed to participate in decision making, provided they are given the proper structure and atmosphere in which to operate. The quality circle describes a small group of employees who work in the same area and who meet on a regular basis with their supervisor to discuss common problems. Problems brought before the group are settled exclusively by the circle. Management does not dictate discussion topics. Once a problem has been identified, the circle formulates a solution and presents it to management, which then decides whether to implement the proposed solution. The style in which management operates is different, but the actual institutional structure remains unchanged.

The success of the quality circles program in industry is well documented. Businesses that have instituted the program have noted a dramatic rise in productivity with a corresponding drop in casual absences, worker complaints, and union grievances. Ouchi (1981) describes two outstanding records of success. The first is the fact that productivity in Japan has increased 400 percent over productivity in the United States for the past three decades. This phenomenal growth cannot be attributed entirely to the quality circle program. However, most experts credit a large share of the success to the positive management-labor relations that they foster. Ouchi further states that the engineers and managers at Buick Final Assembly in Flint, Michigan did not feel that the program would work with the more independent and militant U.S. worker. However, since their plant was in danger of being closed because of years of poor performance, they were willing to experiment, and a quality circle program was implemented with the cooperation of the United Auto Workers (UAW). When the program began, Buick Final Assembly had one of the lowest levels of efficiency and quality in the entire corporation. Within two years, the plant had risen to first rank among all General Motors assembly plants in quality and efficiency. The UAW was equally impressed with the improvement in the work environment.

When is an organization ready for a quality circles program? Cleary and others (1982) believe that institutions that face difficult times as a result not of their own ineffectiveness but of external pressures are excellent candidates for a quality circle program. These conditions indicate that most higher education institutions are prime candidates for such programs.

Shared Governance

The ultimate success of the management-faculty relationship will be little affected by how it is named. Hence, a name should be chosen that is not emotionally charged. The term *quality circle* is closely associated with corporate management systems, and its use should be avoided. Words that remind members of past institutional failures should also be avoided. The implementation of a new program will be difficult enough without having to argue false issues. Hence, for the purposes of this discussion, the quality circle concept will be termed *shared governance.*

Shared governance is hardly a new concept. A decade ago, Richardson and others (1972, p. 185) argued for the program: "Campus structure should reflect a genuine desire to share power among the various constituencies. Each constituency must have the opportunity of influencing action at each level where decisions are made affecting their interests."

A Need to Change. The first prerequisite for changing the working relationship between management and faculty is a felt need to do so. Usually, this step originates with a top administrator. A number of internal and external factors can generate this need. Whether the idea originates with management or faculty, the next step is clear: Top leadership from the affected faculty groups must be involved. Nothing will kill the program more quickly than the union's perception that the administration is starting a competing faculty group.

The beginning steps should then be carefully planned. Only a few key members of the administration, union, and senate should be involved. Participants must include at least the presidents of the respective groups. If the commitment is not present at the top, it is not likely to found elsewhere. The only agenda item should be an interest-level discussion to discover whether a continuation of the process is desirable.

Role of the Consultants. If the decision is made to continue, the advice of an outside consultant should be sought. If such expertise is available on campus, it should be rejected promptly. The consultant must be free from knowledge of campus personalities and historical grievances between the parties. Further, neither management nor faculty should feel that they are being lectured to by the other party, a common trait among educators. The consultant should make available readings on successfully run shared governance programs, and visits to the successful institutions should be arranged at the onset of the program.

The next meeting should include from twelve to fifteen leaders from the various groups. It is important at this early stage not to involve overly negative people. If a new and sensitive program is to be tried fairly, its early participants must be committed to success. The meeting should be conducted by the consultant with the goal of creating a caring and trusting relationship between the participants. If an adversarial relationship has been the norm for many years, this will be a difficult but crucial step in the process.

Formation of the Steering Committee. As the relationship moves from need and commitment to planning and implementation, it will become necessary to form a steering committee. The committee, which should remain small, should include key members from the faculty and administration. The primary objective of the steering committee is to spread support and commitment over a large number of people. The design and function of the committee is depicted in Figure 1. The committee's objective is to promote the mission of the college and an improved quality of work life through the shared governance structure. It has three functions: to advise the college president on all governance issues, to encourage and support the shared governance structure, and to identify problems and develop techniques for resolving them.

The steering committee should meet at least once a month and, to the extent possible, away from campus. An off-campus environment contributes to friendly, relaxed, and open discussions. It also lessens the faculty perception that the administration is now in charge. Confidence building is a slow process, and it should not be rushed. It may take one to two years before the shared governance structure moves beyond the steering committee. During this period, its primary function should be to develop problem-solving techniques involving management and faculty.

Suppose, for example, that the president of the college receives notification that the state is to decrease the college's appropriated funding by 10 percent. The problem is brought before the steering committee with an explanation of the possible consequences. The group's response might be to form an ad hoc budget committee whose members represent management, union, senate, and perhaps other

Figure 1. Steering Committee

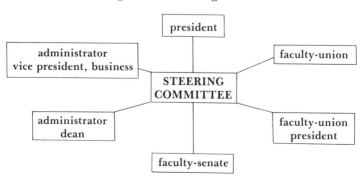

campus interests. The charge of the committee would be to formulate a plan and to advise the college president on a course of action. The faculty leadership has been involved with the problem from the very beginning and therefore must share some responsibility for its resolution and eventual acceptance by the full faculty.

A second and more typical approach for solving the same problem would be for central administration to evaluate the impact of decreased funding and implement its solution through lower management levels. At first, faculty would be involved at the department level, with each department demanding that it be spared the cuts. Senate discussion would be hostile and accusatory, with members blaming each other and management for fiscal irresponsibility and complaining that they were accorded too little importance in the overall operation of the institution. When the budget cuts were finally made, the union would at last be involved, probably through the grievance procedure. This all too common situation represents the adversarial relationship at its worst.

The steering committee must resist the temptation to resolve issues within the group. This may be difficult since so many of the college's leaders will be meeting around the same table. However, the committee will become just another level of college bureaucracy if it does not keep as its main goal the spread of the shared governance concept to all levels of management and faculty.

A Collegewide Model. Implementation of the final stage of the structure is the most difficult, because many more people are involved; hence, the committee must be greater. However, the increased involvement will lessen the impact of the loss of one or two key individuals.

Figure 2 shows how the model might look at a community college. A number of arrangements are possible. However, the groups should remain relatively small, with five to six faculty members and two to

Figure 2. Collegewide Committee Model

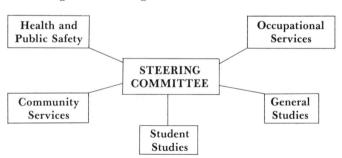

three administrators. Each area should encompass more than one department, as most campuses already suffer from excessive departmentalization. Care must also be taken that administrators do not represent too many areas. All areas will be similar to the occupational model depicted in Figure 3. The objective is to facilitate the working relationship and communication links between the faculty, department heads, union, senate, and administration. Each area committee has three functions: to identify problems, to address recommendations for resolving the problems to the current management-faculty structure, and to advise the steering committee. Thus, the role of the area committees is similar to that of the steering committee, except that their members are more involved in problem resolution. The committees do not replace any part of the existing institutional structure. Rather, they allow for joint deliberation on all governance issues. Discussion topics can include budget considerations, faculty and course schedules, instructional services, program evaluation, faculty and administrative evaluation, and professional development.

Objections certainly will be made to the inclusion of the union so directly in the day-to-day operation of the institution. Thus, it is again worth noting that at many community colleges the union is the only source of legitimate faculty leadership, and it is capable of representing the faculty on all governance issues. Further, Clark (1981) suggests that unions already are involved in governance through the grievance process and that this involvement is increasing. The grievance procedure is time-consuming and costly, and it intensifies the adversarial relationship between faculty and management. In the final analysis, shared governance is advisory to administration and should pose little threat.

At this point in the process, the shared governance structure is ready for expansion to include all campus groups. The expanded struc-

Figure 3. Area Committee

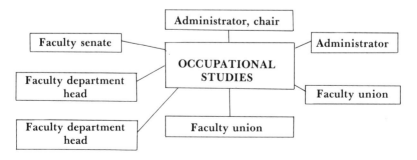

ture will resemble the quality circles model in industry, with each major area represented by a separate steering committee. All employees should be involved in a circle in their particular work area on a voluntary basis. One such steering committee could be chaired by the director of buildings and grounds and include two supervisors, two union leaders, three employees, and a faculty member acting as liaison with the total self-governance structure. To avoid potential conflict, members from two different unions should probably not serve on the same steering committee. Students could be represented by their own steering committee; chaired by the dean of students, it could include a financial aids officer, a department head, an interested faculty member, and several students. The faculty member could act as liaison with the entire structure. An annual picnic, retreat, or other college activity could be planned with all steering committee members invited. Staff involvement in the operation of and concern for the institution must be enhanced by implementation of such a program.

Conclusion

The success or failure of shared governance depends on the commitment of many key individuals and campus groups. Thus, it faces many threats. Cleary and others (1982) point out that one of the major stumbling blocks to the success of the program is acceptance by lower-level management, who often are promoted and remunerated on the basis of performance goals in their area; consequently, they feel that they must be in constant control of any situation. They operate in a competitive environment, and they are unaccustomed to the spirit of cooperation. Ouchi (1981, p. 113) also suggests that the manager's job will not become easier under a shared governance system: "The managers will doubt their personal skill at management, question the coordinate skill of their subordinates, and feel unsure about being a manager. In the short run, a manager in an autocratic system has more pleasures."

Union members are apt to be equally recalcitrant. Some will suspect management's every advance as an attempt to undermine union authority. Members will enter meetings with hidden agendas and with a phobia about giving something away before the next round of negotiations. Further, as suggested earlier, unions may not wish to become involved in issues where they have so little to gain. However, the record of shared governance programs has been excellent. In industry, productivity and quality of work life goals have made spectacular gains under such models. At Washtenaw Community College (WCC) in

Ann Arbor, Michigan, management and faculty have been experimenting with such a program for more than two years. While the results are not spectacular, they are notable. Before involvement in the shared governance program, union and management at WCC annually processed a number of arbitration cases. During the past two years, not one case has been filed, although some critical issues have been confronted. Several senate-style concerns have also been solved through management-faculty involvement precipitated by the steering committee. The union at WCC is the only representative faculty group.

Shared governance is not a panacea that instantly can solve every problem that an organization faces. It works only if there is total commitment to a trusting, caring, and cooperative relationship based on the realization that we face difficult times. And, we must face them together. Institutions that adapt to changing conditions will survive well into the future.

References

Baldridge, J. V., Kemerer, F. R., Adams, B., Najita, J., Naples, C., Schlesinger, S., and Thompson, J. "Assessing the Impact of Faculty Collective Bargaining." *American Association of Higher Education,* ERIC/Higher Education Research Report, no. 8, 1981, 1–57.

Carnegie Council on Higher Education. *Three Thousand Futures: The Next Twenty Years for Higher Education.* San Francisco: Jossey-Bass, 1980.

Clark B. "Arbitration in American Higher Education." Unpublished doctoral dissertation, Vanderbilt University, 1981.

Cleary, M., Amsden, D. M., and Amsden, R. T. "The Quality Circle Process: The ASQC Model for Success." In *Management by Japanese Systems.* New York: Praeger, 1982.

Douglas, M. "A Study of the Role and Responsibilities of the Academic Senate and the California Teacher's Association Bargaining Unit in Educational Matters." Unpublished doctoral dissertation, Pepperdine University, 1980.

Garbarino, J. *Faculty Bargaining.* New York: McGraw-Hill, 1975.

Hankin, J. N. "State Legislatures and the Status of Collective Bargaining in Community and Junior Colleges." 1976–77 Special Report, no. 28. Washington, D.C.: Academic Collective Bargaining Information Service, 1976. (ED 129 387)

Johnstone, R. *The Scope of Faculty Bargaining.* Westport, Conn.: Greenwood Press, 1981.

Julius, D. J. "Collective Bargaining in Higher Education: The First Decade." A paper for the American Association for Higher Education, Washington, D.C., 1977.

Kelley, E. P., Jr., and Rodriguez, R. L. "Observations on Collective Bargaining: Implications for Academic Management." *Liberal Education,* 1977, *43* (1), 102–117.

Kemerer, F. R., and Baldridge, J. V. "Senates and Unions: Unexpected Peaceful Coexistence." *Journal of Higher Education,* 1981, *52* (3), 256–263.

Lieberman, M. "Faculty Senates: A Dissenting View." Paper presented at the 24th national conference of the American Association for Higher Education, Chicago, March 1969.

Mayhew, L. B. *Surviving the Eighties: Strategies and Procedures for Solving Fiscal and Enrollment Problems.* San Francisco: Jossey-Bass, 1979.

Minzey, J. D. "Eureka! Dai-jo-bu! Amazing!" *Michigan School Board Journal,* October 1982, p. 24.

Ouchi, W. G. *Theory Z: How American Business Can Meet the Japanese Challenge.* Reading, Mass.: Addison-Wesley, 1981.

Richardson, R. C., Jr., Blocker, C. E., and Bender, L. W. *Governance for the Two-Year College.* Englewood Cliffs, N.J.: Prentice-Hall, 1972.

Dennis W. Bila is a mathematics instructor at Washtenaw Community College in Ann Arbor, Michigan; former president of the Washtenaw Community College Education Association; and the author of a number of mathematics textbooks.

*To paraphrase Peter Drucker, a strategic plan is a collection
of today's decisions that will shape tomorrow's college.
Strategic planning is a process that articulates the best
thinking of those involved in creating and implementing
institutional strategies.*

Strategic Planning

Warren H. Groff

During the past three decades, community colleges focused on developing programs and acquiring resources and facilities for constantly
increasing numbers of students. Staff energies were devoted to the
immediate needs of instruction and service and minimum regard was
paid to the long-term future. During the late 1970s, enrollment in community colleges began to stabilize, and for the first time these institutions began to experience extended periods of financial constraint.
Community college leaders came to realize that their future could no
longer be shaped simply by reacting to immediate student needs. The
colleges began to institute planning processes that would enable them
to anticipate the impact of demographic, economic, social, and political
forces in their external environment and to establish priorities for the
use of limited resources. In fact, planning concepts emerged in all areas
of postsecondary education. The Council of Independent Colleges, the
Academy for Educational Development, and the American Association
of State Colleges and Universities launched programs relating to comprehensive institutional planning. These projects and others like them
all stressed the need to assess the external environment and to anticipate the impact of external trends on the institution.

G. A. Myran (Ed.). *Strategic Management in the Community College.* New Directions
for Community Colleges, no. 44. San Francisco: Jossey-Bass, December 1983.

Definition of Strategic Planning

According to Steiner (1979), strategic planning is a backbone support to strategic management. It is not the entirety of strategic management, but it is a major process in the conduct of strategic management. Planning provides a framework for integrated decision making throughout the organization. At the strategic level, long-range comprehensive plans are developed to achieve overall missions. Short-range plans are used at the operating level and implemented through detailed tactics.

Peters (1979, p. 25) defines strategic planning as "a process that directs an organization's attention to the future, thereby enabling the organization to adapt more readily to change. The major contribution of the planning process to good management is the rationality it imposes on an organization's efforts to anticipate its future. Creative organizations are able to examine the basic assumptions under which they operate and to adapt them to new situations. Creativity is a basic tool for good planning and not some poetic appendage to the process." Thieme (1979, p. 26) states: "Real strategic planning does not start with assumptions about institutional mission. Mission can only be realistically set after a careful assessment of the external environment and the internal strengths and weaknesses of the institution and after identification of practical options."

Strategic planning can be generally described as a process that follows a number of sequential steps. Figure 1 depicts these steps.

In the community college setting, strategic planning can be defined as an objective methodology based on external assessment and internal audit for formulating a set of decisions about what the college will become in the future.

This chapter will review the strategic elements of an institutional plan: assessment of the external environment, ways of auditing institutional strengths and weaknesses, and ways of matching institutional or system strengths with opportunities in the external environment through the process of strategic goal setting.

Assessing the External Environment

Institutions and systems need the capacity to collect and analyze information on a broad range of variables in the external environment in order to develop a desirable and feasible future. The variables that can be assessed include those listed in Table 1.

One example of a tool that can be used to assess the external

Figure 1. Steps of Strategic Management

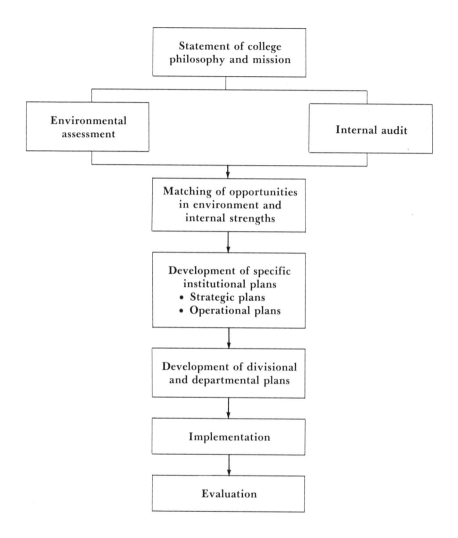

environment is the future-creating paradigm of the American Association of State Colleges and Universities (1978). The paradigm uses a cross-influence matrix of eleven societal trends and twelve values to determine goals in ten areas. The eleven societal trends are population, government, global affairs, environment, energy, economy, science and technology, human settlements, work, life-style, women, and participation. The twelve societal values are change, freedom, equality, leisure, foresight, pluralism, localism, responsibility, knowledge, quality,

Table 1. Sample Subcategories and Suggested Data Categories

Demographic Characteristics	Economic Trends	Social Indicators
Population size	Textile industry	Population and the family
Age distribution	Auto industry	Health and nutrition
Sex ratio	Electronics industry	Housing and the environment
Marital status	Telecommunications industry	Transportation
Ethnic and cultural characteristics	Health care industry	Public safety
Education levels	Agriculture industry	Education and training
Economic status	Airline industry	Work patterns
Population density	Energy industry	Social security and welfare
Degree of urbanization	Steel industry	Income and productivity
Racial composition	Insurance industry	
Unemployment	Shipbuilding industry	Social participation
Poverty and deprivation	Biotechnology industry	Culture, leisure, and use of time
Illiteracy	Aerospace industry	
Existence of basic community services	Defense industry	
Social, political, economic well-being	Synfuel industry	
	Mining industry	
	Education industry	

goals, and interdependence. The ten goals are finance, students, research and development, public service, facilities, faculty, curricula, administration, resources, and athletics. Van Ausdale (1980) uses several of these variables in documents that will be useful to institutions that wish to develop planning processes that track numerous changes.

Other tools for assessing the external environment include market analysis, environmental scanning, and trend analysis. Market analysis consists of obtaining detailed information about markets or market segments served or unserved by an institution or system. Market analysis is an organized effort to identify the relationship between specific wants and needs of people and the ways in which institutions meet or could meet them through a coherent plan of research, strategy, and communication. Environmental scanning consists of sampling data for a wide range of sources as they relate to a specific area, such as unemployment. Trend analysis consists of a systematic review of comparable data over time to determine direction.

Data are the foundation on which a multiyear institutional plan can be built. They are also the basis on which institutions are managed or evaluated. In the past, management information systems have tended to focus on data elements relating to internal operations of the institution, such as registration, scheduling, class rosters, space utilization, grade reporting, student aid, payroll, budgeting, and other administrative applications. In the past, data have been collected and grouped in files labeled *students, personnel, finance,* and *space.* Although the processing of data elements that are essentially internal to the institution will continue to be an important factor in decision making, organizational strategic planning processes are becoming increasingly more dependent on data elements external to the institution. Management information systems of the future will include the integration of internal and external data sets.

Auditing the Internal Environment

An internal audit of an institution or system should be as objective as possible. Objectivity is made possible by developing specific criteria for assessing each college function and by involving a broad range of persons in the assessment process. Persons involved in the assessment process can evaluate each function. For example, if a single institution uses a president's cabinet and several other persons to assess the capability of the college to assess its external environment, each person can independently evaluate the college relative to needs assessment, market analysis, trend analysis, and environmental scanning. The evaluations of independent auditors can reveal a great deal of useful information. Once several selected persons have audited a college function, there is great benefit to a process of dialogue to determine whether there is consensus on the rating of the function. Ultimately, the objectives of this process are to determine the extent to which each function can contribute to the college's future and to develop specific strategies and plans related to that function. Because most resources are in direct support of certificate, degree, and diploma programs, evaluation of these programs deserves special attention. They can be evaluated on the basis of quality and market viability. Quality is a function of faculty, students, library holdings, support services, program characteristics, program advisory committees, and other variables. Market viability is defined in relation to demand in the marketplace, competition, and comparative advantage. Assessment of the external environment can provide insights into dimensions of market viability.

Setting Goals

The purpose of external assessment and internal audit is to gain insights that will help the institution to choose strategic goals and chart a course of action over the next several years. The results of the external assessment should consist of a listing of opportunities and threats, in rank order to the extent possible. These opportunities and threats can be judged to be primarily demographic, economic, social, or political. The results of the internal audit should yield a list of strengths and weaknesses, also in rank order to the extent possible. This process of listing and ranking the external and internal conditions that will have an impact on the future of the college completes the assessment phase of strategic planning, and the goal-setting process begins. Strategic goal setting focuses more on the what of the future than on the how, so the technology of long-range planning (establishing program objectives, setting budget objectives, developing timelines, making assignments to individual staff members for implementation, and so forth) will not be addressed here. There are scores of excellent handbooks available to those who wish to pursue the development of long-range plans for their college. The objective of strategic goal setting is to create a framework for study, dialogue, and decision making that will produce a set of goals or decisions that express the basic strategies to be followed in creating the preferred institution of the future. Once these strategic decisions have been made, the development of long-range and short-range plans will provide the blueprint needed to ensure that these strategies are carried out. For the purpose of this discussion, the process of goal setting will be divided into two phases: development of assumptions and development of strategic goals.

Development of Assumptions. The statement of assumptions is the critical link between the analysis of external and internal conditions and the development of strategic goals. The development of assumptions forces college staff to analyze these conditions and to express their concrete implications for the college. Once the assumptions have been stated, it is no longer necessary to refer back to the statements of external and internal conditions in developing goal statements, since the assumption statements provide an important bridge between conditions and goal statements.

An assumption can be described as a proposition describing future conditions over which the institution has little control and which will have an impact on its future. The level of certainty assigned to an assumption determines the level of precision that it is allowed in subsequent planning. The greater the uncertainty about the assumption, the greater must be the range of flexibility that the institution retains to prepare for the assumed condition. Raising the certainty level of an assumption yields greater planning precision, better long-term goals effectiveness, and improved cost efficiency and program effectiveness. Here are two examples of assumptions for an individual community: It is assumed that the seventeen- to twenty-four-year-old population in the college's service area will decline by 10 percent during the next five years and that the thirty-five- to forty-five-year-old population will increase by 20 percent. It is assumed that the need for short-term job upgrading programs tailored for specific employee groups of area businesses and industry will increase dramatically. Categories for specifying assumptions by a specific college could include societal context, quality of life and quality of worklife issues, human resource development needs, and capital funding needs.

Development of Strategic Goals. The development of strategic institutional goals is the culminating step in strategic planning. Strategic goals can be viewed as a collection of today's decisions to shape tomorrow's college. Strategic goal statements tend to be quite general, whereas objectives contained in operational plans must by necessity be specific and time-bound. Here are two examples of strategic goals: The college will increase the percentage of human and financial resources devoted to improvement of programs and service quality by 10 percent over a two-year period. The college will expand programs and services related to economic development and job training by focusing additional resources on short-term tailored programs for area employers.

It should be emphasized that the greatest benefit of the strategic goal-setting process comes from the staffwide deliberation required to develop the goal statements. This process produces among staff groups needed consensus, commitment, and understanding of institutional priorities. Staff deliberations and goal setting will tend to center around some of the key strategic opportunities and issues facing community colleges today: program quality, economic development and job training, recruitment of new student clientele, retention of present students, diversification of instructional design, and retrenchment.

Conclusion

The future of our community colleges cannot be predicted, but it is possible to use our anticipatory and speculative skills to improve our foresight. Much can be known about the future, just as much can be known about the past. Strategic planning processes involve the institutional assessment, study, dialogue, and goal-setting processes that will shape the best future for the college.

For example, the future of the community college depends on our ability to anticipate changes in the workplace. In testimony before the House Subcommittee on Elementary, Secondary, and Vocational Education, Richard Wilson (1982), representing the American Association of Community and Junior Colleges, made several points that colleges must consider as they make strategic decisions regarding their role in economic development and job training: "The future of our nation depends on how fully we utilize our human resources. As our economy becomes more dependent on high technology and the delivery of sophisticated services, the need for better development of our human resources is a necessity. Only well-educated and competently trained people can master the new technologies and specialized services that are increasingly in demand. The future of vocational education will depend on how well it satisfies the interests and demands of adult students. The demographic data are clear. The school age population... declined 11 percent in the 1970s, and another 10 percent decline is forecast for the 1980s. Another significant factor is frequent career changes caused by technological developments and the creation of new markets, products, and services. Nowadays, it is common for individuals to develop, use, and replace career skills three or more times before they eventually retire from full-time employment."

The college that assesses changing conditions in the local labor market, that audits internal strengths and areas for improvement in relation to these changing conditions, that makes assumptions about how these external and internal conditions will affect the institutional future, and that then develops strategic goals based on the insights provided by the assessment, audit, and assumption-making processes will certainly be better prepared to thrive in a turbulent environment than a less planful and future-oriented college. Community colleges can drift into the future, or they can take action-oriented, dynamic, purposeful steps to shape the best institutional future. The choice is ours.

References

American Association of State Colleges and Universities. *A Future-Creating Paradigm.* Washington, D.C.: Resource Center for Planned Change, 1978.

Peters, J. P. "Four Challenges to Effective Long-Range Planning." *Trustee,* American Hospital Association, 1979, *46*, 25–27.

Steiner, G. A. *Strategic Planning.* New York: Macmillan, 1979.

Thieme, C. W. "Strategic Planning Market Orientation." *Hospitals: Journal of the American Hospital Association,* 1979, *32*, 25–27.

Van Ausdale, S. *Comprehensive Institutional Planning in Two-Year Colleges.* Columbus, Ohio: National Center for Research in Vocational Education, 1980.

Wilson, R. Testimony before the U.S. House of Representatives Subcommittee on Elementary, Secondary, and Vocational Education, July 22, 1982. Available in the U.S. Congressional Record.

Warren H. Groff is vice president for academic affairs at North Central Technical College in Mansfield, Ohio. He serves as chairperson of the Ohio Board of Regents Chancellor's Task Force on High Technology.

Given the interrelationship between institutional goals and financial resources, it follows that an organization's future can be no more certain than its finances. The strategic manager must therefore strive to bring the highest degree of certainty into the financial plans of the college.

Strategic Elements of Financial Management

Albert L. Lorenzo

To say that executive-level managers in higher education are currently facing tremendous pressures may be a serious understatement of the facts. The impact of demographics, taxpayer attitudes, and reduced governmental allocations is enough to weary even the best administrators. But, despite these severe limitations on resources, people expect executive-level managers to keep the institution dynamic and alive. Although it now requires herculean effort to achieve it, fiscal stability is still the expected norm, and only continued progress and innovation bring any praise. Stated more simply, although the conditions affecting institutions of higher education have changed dramatically, what is expected of their managers remains the same. Drucker (1980, p. 9) recognized the changes being called for during such turbulent times and suggests that, as these difficult periods arise, "the fundamentals have to be managed, and managed well."

Like their counterparts in the private sector, institutions of higher education are assemblies of three basic resources: human, physical, and fiscal. The manager's principal responsibility is to orchestrate these resources in the most efficient manner while attaining organizational goals. The fact that the three basic resources cannot be viewed as discrete complicates this task considerably. That is, management ineffectiveness in any one area will diminish results in the others.

G. A. Myran (Ed.). *Strategic Management in the Community College.* New Directions for Community Colleges, no. 44. San Francisco: Jossey-Bass, December 1983.

Sound fiscal management has long been identified as a basic requirement for institutional growth and development, and poor financial management is the quickest path to disaster. As a result, the years have produced scores of well-tested guides and systems for good fiscal planning and control. Whether the method that is chosen is manual or automated and whether it is maintained on pegboards or sophisticated computers, a sound system of financial accounting and management must be in place before any new directions are initiated.

Drucker (1980, p. 9) argues that "fundamentals do not change. But, the specifics to manage them do change greatly with changes in internal and external conditions." Perhaps this concept best describes why the emphasis on the strategic elements of financial management is now increasing. In general, fundamental financial management encompasses the basic systems for budgeting, recording, and controlling transactions as well as for reporting the results of operations. In contrast, strategic financial management involves the resource-oriented actions and decisions that consider the relationship between the college and its environment and that shape the future of the organization.

The nature and the abundance of financial resources are critical determinants of an organization's future. However, Mann (1979) points out that financial planners at community colleges face numerous uncertainties. Given the interrelationship between institutional goals and financial resources, it follows that an organization's future can be no more certain than its finances. The strategic manager must therefore strive to bring the highest degree of certainty into the financial plans of the college.

Growth and Maturity

Plans for shaping the future begin with a realistic understanding of current conditions. Like human beings, organizations can grow and develop differently. Thus, a critical examination of where a college is today and of what caused it to be that way is one prerequisite for considering a college's future. The two factors most closely tied to financial planning are growth and maturity.

Potential Versus Inclination to Grow. Although humans and organizations share many development characteristics, organizations have a distinct advantage. They can choose their ultimate size, and under most conditions they can even choose to change their size if that appears to be desirable. In making the choice, managers must first debate whether the organization has the potential to grow; then they must decide whether it has the inclination to do so.

Evaluating growth potential is not always as easy as it first appears, especially in an open-door environment. Every community college keeps accurate records of all students who enroll, but few colleges are able to capture reliable data on students who are turned away or who elect reduced loads. In the absence of such information, decision makers are forced to rely on estimates and best guesses.

Growth potential can be evaluated in two ways. The first assesses the ability of the college to expand courses and programs currently being offered. The second assesses the likelihood of attracting students from new markets. Generally, expanding current offerings is more desirable, since it is both less costly and less risky than developing an array of new products to serve an unexplored market.

If managers satisfy themselves that growth is possible, they must then decide whether growth is desirable. This decision may have to rely more on good judgment than on quantitative data. The factors to be considered will vary by institution, but they generally will relate to plant capacity, recruitment capability, efficiency of operations at current size, and availability of resources to support growth. In any event, it is clear that growth cannot occur unless both factors are present, that is, unless the college has both the potential and the inclination to grow.

Indications of Maturity. Organizational maturity has absolutely nothing to do with chronology. Moreover, the mere passage of time can give false impressions that an institution has matured. The first sign of maturity is the absence of growth, not just in enrollment but in plant and staffing as well.

Unfortunately, most Americans equate growth with success. As a result, the first reactions to organizational maturity are usually negative. Actually, the beginnings of maturity can be a real blessing to growth-weary administrators and faculty who have spent years trying to keep pace with a constantly expanding operation. Maturity can provide the first real opportunity to concentrate on what the college has become — and, more importantly, on what it should be.

Since maturity is related to growth and since organizations have the ability to control their own growth, the quickest way to reach maturity is simply to decide to stop growing. For colleges whose growth curve has been quite steep, that may be the wisest decision that they ever make. In order to approximate where an organization is on its maturity curve, the organization can assess the degree of completion of a number of tangible elements relative to its master plan. For example, what percent of the total number of full-time staff who will probably ever be employed are now at work? How complete are the physical facilities? How many new programs will be added to the curriculum? How much is already in place? The higher the percentage of completion in these and other categories, the more mature the college has become.

Impact of Growth on Financing. In the past, growth not only implied success, it virtually assured financial well-being. New resources came from increased tax bases, student fees, and state aid, as the populations of districts and colleges grew simultaneously. Recent events have changed much of that, so many institutions now find that the open door admits additional students who must be educated within existing resource levels.

The long-standing business axiom about making it up on volume applied to community colleges as well. As these institutions grew, the fixed costs of the district were spread over a larger base, and resulting economies occurred. More growth meant more economies, so growth was encouraged. Soon, however, the increased size diminished responsiveness to student and community needs, so additional layers of support staff and administration were approved and brought on line. The added costs that resulted threatened efficiency and for the first time caused community colleges to question whether there was a limit to economies of size.

It is difficult to say precisely when economies of scale become diseconomies. The exact point depends on the unique characteristics of a given institution. Drucker (1980, p. 63) suggests a range where this might typically occur: "There may also be an upper limit to the optimal size in higher education in America. Above 8,000 or 10,000 students, there are no more economies of scale and increasing diseconomies."

The point of diminishing return can also be approximated by carefully studying fixed and variable cost patterns and by monitoring the relationship between marginal revenue and marginal expense. Generally, if a new increment of growth provides more new revenue than the related direct cost, economies will continue to accrue from growth. At the same time, attention must be paid to the fixed cost layer—physical plant; support staff in areas such as purchasing, accounting, data processing, admissions, and records; and insurance. At some point, new growth increments will increase fixed costs. When the increase in fixed costs plus the marginal expenses exceeds new incremental revenue, diseconomies begin to set in.

Impact of Maturity on Financing. Ideally, as managers begin to sense that their college is nearing maturity, they should manage growth more carefully. Having determined somewhat by accident what an institution's maximum size is, demographics and economics can force a quick search for what the optimum size should be. Often, the optimum size proves to be at a level slightly below maximum size.

If the last layers of growth were carefully planned, they would not have produced any increase in the fixed cost base. Similarly, no permanent resources would have been added that could not be easily removed. If reducing enrollment slightly will result in better overall efficiency, then the reduction can take place without inflicting major trauma on the organization. A strategic financial manager's goal should therefore be to plan for growth near maturity to allow for rapid scaling back should it become necessary to reduce size in order to increase overall efficiency.

Another change resulting from maturity is a diminished emphasis on traditional capital outlay funding. Once facilities are constructed, equipment is purchased, and sites are developed, the amount of attention given to financing these activities will decline. However, the need to fund repair, renovation, and equipment replacement programs will soon become a high priority for the mature college. Strategic financial managers must give early consideration to this change of emphasis in fund requirements.

Finally, a mature institution will not be able to rely on excess revenue from growth to finance new ventures. Instead, new programs will draw resources away from existing lower-priority programs. Reallocation of resources will become the strategic manager's principal source of funding for innovation and change as the institution reaches the upper end of its growth and maturity curves.

Enabling Characteristics

Each organization must assess its readiness for a shift into a more strategic form of financial management. As mentioned previously, the fundamentals must be well managed. This not only presumes that a sound system of financial accounting and reporting is solidly in place but that the systems are managed by professionals who have adequate technical skills to produce the outcomes usually associated with such systems.

Accuracy, timeliness, and utility are key indicators of a sound fundamental financial operation. For example, any college that must wait for its auditors to determine whether the prior year produced a surplus or deficit clearly is not ready to become strategic in its approach to financial management. Similarly, inaccuracies, tardiness, or poor formatting make reports of operations, especially at the cost center and division levels, of little value to unit managers; energy would best be spent correcting those deficiencies before steps to initiate strategic management are taken.

However, having the financial house in order is only one pre-condition for successful strategic endeavors. A complete and updated mission statement is just as important. Since the goal of strategic management is to shape the institution's future, a contemporized mission statement acts in the same way as a compass for an explorer. The mission statement points the general direction and warns of deviations from the preferred path.

The mission statement for most community colleges sets forth a far larger array of ideal outcomes than can possibly be achieved with the resources generally available. Consequently, it is used as a legitimizing agent, stipulating in broadest terms the types of programs and services deemed acceptable to offer. However, since resources are limited, it may be useful to prioritize the mission statement, placing greatest emphasis on the portions that permit the most desirable results. Clear priorities will aid in planning and resource reallocation efforts.

Setting priorities on mission requires some difficult decisions to be made. Competing ideas will surface, and special-interest groups will form. Thus, courage is another characteristic that aids a strategic environment in the governance of an institution. If top executive officers and governing boards cannot withstand the pressure or if they place political expediency ahead of practical needs, the process of strategic management is doomed to failure.

A final characteristic that will allow managers to become more strategic is credibility, at least on the macro level. Wildavsky (1979) underscores the need for confidence as a basic ingredient in the budgetary and financial planning process. Fundamental management deals with elements that are far more tangible than those involved in strategic techniques. If management's credibility and confidence are low when discussing conclusions supported by facts and quantitative data, management will be in serious difficulty when it seeks support for plans based principally on judgment.

Viewing the College

Private enterprise must earn the right to remain in existence. In contrast, many public organizations seem to presume that, because of the inherent value of the product or service that they offer, they have the right to remain in existence. This basic difference of philosophy can have a profound impact on the attitudes and practices of public sector managers. Community college administrators may be wise to examine practices in place in private sector industries. In fact, Leslie and Miller

(1974) argue that during difficult times colleges act very much like their business counterparts by seeking innovations that will permit them to maintain their market position. Some of these innovations relate to increasing enrollments, while others are targeted at finding additional resources. Community college administrators interested in becoming more entrepreneurial in their approach should give thought to the areas of market orientation, product orientation, institutional positioning, and the realities of economic vulnerability.

Market orientation in the traditional sense includes a variety of elements not germane to strategic management since they are operational in nature. Of importance are those elements that require the manager to examine the environment surrounding the college carefully and to extract key indicators of changing needs. There are two extremes in marketing. At one extreme, a product is developed. Then resources are invested in convincing people that they need it. As need is perceived, sales increase. The opposite approach calls for investing resources in determining which needs exist, then in developing products that meet those needs. All that remains is to inform people of product availability, and sales will result. Clearly, the second approach is more strategic.

Product orientation is much like market orientation, only it is concentrated internally. Everything offered by a community college for a price, whether the price is paid by the consumer or by a third party, can be defined as a product. Products can be new or long-standing, the institution can be offering them in competition with others or somewhat exclusively, and they may be selling or not. One way of understanding products is to examine the concept of product life cycle. A classic description of how an industrialist can exploit the product life cycle is offered by Levitt (1965), who shows that most successful products pass through four recognizable stages: development, growth, maturity, and decline. The similarity to the pattern discussed earlier for organizations is remarkable. Such congruity should not be surprising, since organizational development is really the aggregation of product performance.

Institutional positioning can be seen as interrelating product and market characteristics in order to achieve the optimum competitive position for an organization. It is considered strategic only if it occurs by design rather than by happenstance. By their very nature, community colleges are well positioned, since they serve a large and constantly growing market segment requiring educational opportunities beyond high school but short of four years. But, being well positioned does not imply freedom from competition. In fact, success often draws competition, as the expanded offerings of high school adult education units and university courses focusing on occupational needs are now showing.

Last, just as the most highly acclaimed figures must admit from time to time that they are only human, community colleges must periodically concede that, despite their success stories, they are vulnerable to economic realities. Failure to view the institution as subject to the same economic pressures that affect private industry can lead to poor decision making and to overconfidence in predicting the success of new ventures.

Sources and Uses of Funds

In 1963, the Accounting Principles Board issued Opinion No. 3, *The Statement of Source and Application of Funds.* The purpose of this supplement to corporate financial reports was to go beyond traditional income statement and balance sheet reporting and provide the reader with insights into where funds were generated and how they were used. In 1971, the Accounting Principles Boards (1971) hailed the acceptance of the statement of source by major stock exchanges and the business community and recommended that, in view of the broadened concept of the funds statement, its title should be changed to "Statement of Changes in Financial Position."

The advent and acceptance of this expanded corporate reporting practice may provide useful guidance to community college managers who wish to become more strategic. Just as the funds statement went beyond balance sheet and income statement considerations, so should strategic financial managers look past assets, liabilities, equities, revenues, and expenditures. That analysis should be handled by competent operational managers. Strategists should strive to determine the reasons for changes in overall financial position and the component sources and uses of funds.

The only remaining task is to change from the accountant's prior period orientation to the strategist's future orientation. In doing this, the manager will devote considerable effort to evaluating the factors that have the greatest potential for financing new directions and to establishing allocation systems that guarantee that resources will be placed to their highest and best use.

Evaluation of Existing Activities

Every enterprise should conduct two efforts continuously and simultaneously: It should study what it should become, and it should study what it now is and should no longer be. That is especially true for community colleges, for, unless conditions change dramatically, the funds to finance new activities and to expand existing activities will come principally from reallocation of existing resources. Richardson (1978, p. 68) emphasizes: "If colleges are to remain adaptive in a period of declining resources, they must change by substitution rather than addition." Outmoded, outdated, and low-output activities will have to be identified, and, if they are found to be of low institutional value, they will have to be curtailed or eliminated to free resources for new ventures.

Without question, the process of identifying items for reduction or elimination yields the highest levels of organizational anxiety and opposition. As a result, the strategic manager will need to design an evaluation system that is as objective and as fair as possible and that can be easily understood by the institution. The strategist must also be certain to apply the model with equal rigor to all areas under review. To do anything less would be seriously to damage the credibility of the decision makers.

A technique frequently used in financial decision making is the cost-benefit analysis. The evaluation can be approached from either side of the equation. That is, holding cost constant, we can ask which alternative produces the greatest benefit; or, if a desired outcome (benefit) is known, we can ask which option has the least cost. In resource allocation decisions, a variation of the constant cost approach is typically used. The analyst compares the levels of benefits being derived from an existing resource commitment with the level of benefit to be derived from the same investment in a new activity.

Cost is usually quite easy to determine. Benefit can be far more difficult to determine. Alfred (1978) outlines a strategy for measuring benefits by designing a classification structure that sets forth broad categories of benefits produced by community colleges that perform a comprehensive educational mission. Each category is then subdivided into detailed data elements with related descriptions of the benefits of community college education in highly specific areas. Another approach to benefit identification is suggested by the results of a study of the outcomes and costs of community college education conducted by Wenckowski (1977). The study did not attempt to address effectiveness but rather identified four major types of desirable benefits that a community college should produce: economic, social, individual, and monetary.

Both the Alfred (1978) and the Wenckowski (1977) methods call for the decision maker to study benefits, but they are benefits that accrue to the student and, in some cases, to the community. To be helpful in reallocation decisions, these methods can be augmented by evaluation of the benefits that accrue to the institution.

Level of Quality. Whatever a college does, it should do well. High quality in individual programs and services is of obvious benefit to students. But, it is also of significant value to the institution — in student recruitment and placement, in staff recruitment and retention, in public relations, and in dozens of other ways. From a financial perspective, quality has two key benefits: It aids in the solicitation of funds, and it insulates against damage resulting from short-term reductions in resources.

Most people appreciate success, and program quality generally connotes success to outside observers. As a result, high-quality offerings are usually the strongest selling points in fund solicitation efforts. Also, when resources decline, some pressure will undoubtedly be felt by all facets of the organization. If program or service quality rates poorly at current expenditure levels, there is no question that any reduction in funding will render the activity worthless. In contrast, programs of high quality should be able to withstand moderate short-term reductions in support and help the college through cyclical downturns in funding. Therefore, there will be a strong correlation between quality and institutional benefit. A search to identify areas of low quality will provide an insight into areas that can be studied further for reallocation possibilities.

Future Potential. While the institutional benefits of an activity may be apparent, we may also ask whether it will be enduring. Just as with quality, there is a direct relationship between the future potential of an activity and its value to the organization. In searching for items to be considered for reallocation, the strategic manager should direct attention to assessing future demand. Understanding the concept of product life cycle discussed earlier will help in making assumptions about the future. In some cases, a decline in demand can be predicted by the pattern of growth that has already occurred.

Unfortunately, few educational institutions invest heavily in sophisticated market analysis techniques. Demand projections are usually linear and extend as trend lines from past events. Since enrollment information is usually the most plentiful source of data, most forecasts are based on the trend of student attendance. While linear trends cannot be ignored, they should be supplemented with more strategic analyses of potential. At a minimum, steps should be taken to determine the present and projected physical size of the markets being served.

Degree of Competition. Just as for private-sector entities, freedom from intense marketplace competition is a significant benefit for institutions in the public sector. Assuming continued demand, minimal competition allows for greater latitude in pricing, requires a smaller investment in advertising and promotion, and generally assures a solid program base. Some sophisticated businesses actually develop a market share strategy. Catry and Chevalier (1980) point out that the attractiveness of a market share position can vary with the nature of competition. Sometimes, a decision to increase market share may be of value in the long run. In other cases, the most sensible solution is to decrease market share, so as to free resources for more profitable ventures. The strategic financial manager will find that understanding the nature of competition for the products of the community college will provide valuable insight into the institutional benefit being received from those products.

Strategic Advantage. Sometimes, the real value of an activity cannot be determined only by a study of its qualitative and quantitative aspects. This is usually the case when the benefit is perceived to be more for the institution's sake than for the sake of its direct outcomes. An example may be afternoon or weekend use of college facilities by high school students in such areas as theater arts or athletics. Continuation of these services is easy to question, because they are seldom cost-justified. At the same time, however, these financially burdened activities may have major benefits in targeted student recruitment efforts.

In determining benefit for the purpose of reallocation, the analyst should apply the test of strategic advantage as a final measure before recommending elimination. To do otherwise could yield short-term advantages that would be more than offset by longer-term losses.

Pricing and Financial Diversification

Even though the principal source of funds for new ventures is reallocation of existing resources, some support will continue to come from more traditional means. The ability of the college to pass along cost increases in the form of some types of price increases will probably be the second greatest source of added funds. Finding new opportunities may well be the third.

Pricing in the higher education environment is no longer a task to be considered lightly. Decreases in governmental support have shifted the burden to students. As price increases, it plays a greater role in the consumer's decision to buy. This is evident as students cite cost as a major reason for transferring from a four-year college to a community college.

Unless financial exigency is the sole factor influencing action, pricing should not be determined by marketplace characteristics alone. Social responsibility and the original purpose of community colleges cannot be ignored. Breneman and Nelson (1981) discuss the principle of equity and its relationship to price. If it is true that community colleges have been chosen as the vehicle to carry out society's stated goal of equal opportunity for postsecondary education, then price should not become a barrier to access. Unfortunately, those elements of society most vocal in support of social responsibility are often the very agencies that have reneged on their own financial commitment.

Another philosophical question relating to pricing is the extent to which costs should be assigned to the direct user. In the past, most program costs were confined to a fairly narrow range. Now, as curriculum for new technologies requires major equipment costs and specialized staff and facilities, managers must decide whether the students in that program should pay the direct cost or whether it should be spread over the entire student body. Imposing new course or laboratory fees aligns with the former thinking, and across-the-board tuition increases imply the latter.

The quest for new resources should not end either. Fundraising efforts, grants, and giving programs are becoming more beneficial as traditional resources diminish. Pursuing nontraditional funding sources also has value for diversifying the college's financial base. As revenue sources are diversified, the institution becomes less dependent on any one source. If one share is adversely affected, it will then have less overall impact on the college's ability to maintain operations.

Resource Allocation

Having assured themselves that funding will be available, either through reallocation, pricing, or diversification of revenue sources, financial managers can focus attention on new allocations. Authorization of new expenditures should correlate to the nature and duration of the revenue source. For example, permanent reductions can be used for permanent additions. However, one-time reductions should not be used for ongoing commitments, such as hiring of new staff.

Some amount of consistency exists between how an organization establishes its goals and how it allocates its resources. Thus, if goal setting is handled in a strategic fashion, resource allocation will also assume a strategic flair. However, most institutions are nonstrategic in both respects, since the most common means of allocating resources in higher education is incremental budgeting (Caruthers and Orwig,

1979). Considering an expansion of the mission statement and conducting market research are two means of becoming more strategic in the resources allocation process.

Expansion of Mission. Budgetary systems cannot be considered strategic unless they follow the declaration of institutional mission and goals. The problem, as stated earlier, is that many mission statements have not been reviewed in years. In reality, although mission is stated in broad terms, it can actually constrain an organization's growth.

A college mission statement is comparable to a corporation's definition of its industry. If the terms are too narrow, progress will be impeded. Levitt (1975) uses the railroads and the Hollywood film companies as examples of self-constraint. Railroad executives defined their industry too narrowly because they were railroad-oriented, not transportation-oriented. Hollywood filmmakers were equally at fault to declare that they were in the movie business, not the entertainment business. In both cases, once extremely profitable industries are now in serious trouble.

Community college executives and governing boards may be the victims of similar myopia. Regardless of how broadly stated institutional missions are, they are almost always expressed in terms of educational outcomes. Asked to define their industry, most community college administrators will be quick to respond: education. The time has come to expand the community college mission and thus for administrators to expand their definition of their industry. Community colleges should cease to perceive themselves as being solely in the business of education. They should restate their mission to encompass all aspects of human development. Such restatement will justify expenditures in vast new fields full of growth potential and allow for creative shaping of the college's future.

Market Research. A wealthy person will suffer very little harm for a small investment error. However, a person on a limited income can seldom afford to make a financial mistake. Community colleges are more typical of people on limited incomes. In selecting areas for new investments, the strategic manager must minimize the risk of being wrong. One way of reducing risk is to rely extensively on market research. Such research, Litten (1980, pp. 43–44) points out, "can also contribute to the more effective provision of educational opportunities to our citizenry through analysis of demographic patterns and projections that identify markets where there is or will be a discrepancy between supply and demand for educational services."

Macomb Community College, which has district offices in Warren, Michigan, has made a major commitment to market research. It relies heavily on public opinion surveys for market and consumer information. A survey undertaken by the college's Center for Community Studies focused on consumer attitudes and on the effect that high unemployment was having on the desire to obtain more education and job skills. The survey found that 13 percent of the district's adults were taking some type of job training or schooling. One third were attending the community college, one fourth were attending a four-year college or university, and the remainder were training at work, at a proprietary school, or with some other type of organization. Center researchers Jacobs and Pritchard (1982) found the indicators of market penetration to be most reliable and noted that the college was proportionately less accommodating to those between the ages of twenty-five and thirty-four, with a larger part of this group going to the four-year college. In contrast, the college dominated both the eighteen to twenty-four-year-old and the forty-five to sixty-four-year-old age groups, with a 50 percent market share of each. The perceived need for training or education among people over age sixty-five was minimal. Moreover, the college was not viewed as serving the needs of management, namely of business owners, managers, supervisors, and public officials, who said that they received most of their training through their employer. Penetration for continuing professional education was low. Finally, the college was meeting the training needs of women better than it was meeting those of men. Obviously, such information as this can be extremely useful in assessing programs and planning new ventures. While there is never a guarantee of success, risk of loss can be lessened by obtaining better market information.

Conclusion

Strategic management involves decisions and actions that attempt to shape the future of the college. Since a community college can only be what it is funded to be, equal efforts must be placed on bringing strategic techniques into the financial management process as well. Understanding organizational growth and maturity will help. Viewing the college in the same manner as a private enterprise will also help. Orientation to both markets and products is essential, so that the college will be able to achieve the optimal competitive position.

Funds to support new ventures will come primarily from reallocation of existing resources, and methods of evaluating institutional benefit will need to be employed. Pricing and diversified revenue sources can also be used to garner additional resources. Allocation systems for new and expanded activities are equally important. Strategic managers should exercise care that the mission statement is current and sufficiently broad, and they should invest in market research in order to minimize risk of loss. In short, the strategic financial manager is a critical partner in the quest for institutional growth and vitality.

References

Accounting Principles Board. *The Statement of Source and Application of Funds.* APB Opinion No. 3. New York: American Institute of Certified Public Accountants, 1963.

Accounting Principles Board. *Reporting Changes in Financial Position.* APB Opinion No. 19. New York: American Institute of Certified Public Accountants, 1971.

Alfred, R. L. (Ed.). *Coping with Reduced Resources.* New Directions for Community Colleges, no. 22. San Francisco: Jossey-Bass, 1978.

Breneman, D. W., and Nelson, S. C. *Financing Community Colleges: An Economic Perspective.* Washington, D.C.: Brookings Institution, 1981.

Caruthers, J. K., and Orwig, M. *Budgeting in Higher Education.* AAHE-ERIC Higher Education Research Report No. 3. Washington, D.C.: American Association for Higher Education, 1979.

Catry, B., and Chevalier, M. "Market Share Strategy and the Product Life Cycle." In R. A. Kerin and R. A. Peterson (Eds.), *Perspectives on Strategic Marketing Management.* Boston: Allyn & Bacon, 1980.

Drucker, P. F. *Managing in Turbulent Times.* New York: Harper & Row, 1980.

Jacobs, J., and Pritchard, B. *Consumer Attitudes: A Public Opinion Survey of Macomb County Residents.* Warren, Mich.: Center for Community Studies, Macomb Community College, 1982.

Leslie, L. L., and Miller, H. F., Jr. *Higher Education and the Steady State.* Washington, D.C.: American Association for Higher Education, 1974.

Levitt, T. "Exploiting the Product Life Cycle." *Harvard Business Review,* 1965, *43* (6), 81–94.

Levitt, T. "Marketing Myopia." *Harvard Business Review,* 1975, *53* (5), 26–48.

Litten, L. H. "Marketing Higher Education: Benefits and Risks for the American Academic System." *Journal of Higher Education,* 1980, *51* (1), 40–59.

Mann, W. J. "Financing Planning and Management: New Strategies." In R. E. Lahti (Ed.), *Managing in a New Era.* New Directions for Community Colleges, no. 28. San Francisco: Jossey-Bass, 1979.

Richardson, R. C., Jr. "Adapting to Declining Resources Through Planning and Research." In R. L. Alfred (Ed.), *Coping with Reduced Resources.* New Directions for Community Colleges, no. 22. San Francisco: Jossey-Bass, 1978.

Wenckowski, C. *Community College Finance Patterns: A Description with an Analysis of the Maryland Finance System.* Columbia, Md.: Howard Community College, 1977.

Wildavsky, A. *The Politics of the Budgetary Process.* Boston: Little, Brown, 1979.

Albert L. Lorenzo is president of Macomb Community College in Warren, Michigan.

The challenge to community colleges is to translate the vision of strategic plans into the reality of programs and services for students.

The Critical Link:
From Plans to Programs

George A. Baker III
Kay McCollough Moore

In one of his numerous incisive observations, Walt Kelly's cartoon character, Pogo, once exclaimed: "We are confronted with insurmountable opportunities!" That statement captures what may be the central, paradoxical predicament of community colleges today: There is no dearth of legitimate needs, worthy goals, or potentially favorable circumstances. Rather, what they lack is the ability to embrace the opportunities, to establish priorities, and to implement the necessary change. In the final analysis, it is through programs and services provided to students that community colleges reflect their commitments and their progress in attaining their goals. Thus, it is through the process of program and service development that the institution identifies opportunities, evaluates their relevance to the institutional mission, distinguishes between what is desirable and what is feasible, and then endeavors to "surmount" its chosen opportunities, removing the barriers between what is and what should be.

A Context for Program and Service Development

As any reasonably alert educator knows, critical and fundamental shifts are occurring in the American society and economy, and

G. A. Myran (Ed.). *Strategic Management in the Community College.* New Directions for Community Colleges, no. 44. San Francisco: Jossey-Bass, December 1983.

colleges are being pressed to cope with their ramifications. Acceleration of technology, shifts in values, economic uncertainties, blurring of sex roles, tightening of resources, changes in demographics — all these factors are altering the fabric of American life. The inexorable change in society creates an imperative need for change in education. That imperative may be strongest for community colleges, precisely because they are — and should be — both in and of their communities. That being the case, they have a dual responsibility: to shape their environment and to be shaped by it.

In times like these, when pressing educational needs are matched in intensity by mounting calls for educational accountability, it is vitally important for institutional change to be purposeful rather than arbitrary or merely expedient. As Martorana and Kuhns (1975, p. 8) assert, "Change for the sake of change — that is, without regard to whether the proposed change will accomplish institutional goals more effectively than current practice — already tends to be the norm. It is unlikely to benefit either institutional survival or student learning and is especially dangerous when the process of change takes the form of reaction to one crisis after another." Colleges can no longer afford the luxury of organizational drift — of decisions made according to exigency or expedience. Long-range strategic planning based on sound information can help the community college to take the initiative in creating its own future.

The Critical Link

Focusing on "the futurity of present decisions" (Drucker, 1970, p. 131), strategic planning encompasses a continuum of activities: determination of long-range institutional goals, adoption of courses of action for achieving those goals, and allocation of resources necessary for goal attainment (Cope, 1978). Most essentially, as Kieft and others (1978, p. xi) have emphasized, "planning is a means for implementing values." It is a process for translating institutional mission and goals into operational programs and services that are supported by available resources in accord with established priorities. Fundamentally, then, community college programs and services must be irrevocably linked to strategic planning on the one hand and to the allocation of resources — people, space, time, and dollars — on the other. Whatever the mission and goals of the college, those aims must finally be reflected in the programs and services that it provides.

The process of program and service development is thus both integral to and an extension of the process of strategic planning. It encompasses not only the initiation of programs and services but also their maintenance, improvement, and expansion — and, alternatively, their curtailment or elimination. It is, in sum, a set of interrelated activities through which the institution assesses its changing relationships with its external environment and internal constituencies and then formulates an appropriate pattern of response.

Six principal elements are the strategic cornerstones for program and service development: institutional mission and goals, student needs and characteristics, community priorities, the values and involvement of internal college constituencies, technology and its impact on educational curriculum and methodology, and financial constraints and political realities.

Institutional Mission and Goals

The establishment of a clear sense of institutional mission is an essential first step toward the development of programs and services and the effective use of resources. Parnell (1981) warns against the hazards of missionlessness by describing a sign observed on a closed office door: *Gone out of business. Didn't know what our business was.* The community college movement is apparently in the midst of an identity crisis. Across the nation, leaders decry the perceived lack of a clear and unified sense of purpose, and discussions about mission are ubiquitous in the literature, the conferences, and the classroom. Richardson (1981) places high priority on the need for mission clarification. Cosand (1979, p. 2) agrees, asserting that "the essential element for community colleges to face up to . . . is the mission of the institutions." Cohen (1980, p. 33) suggests that there is some difficulty in identifying community colleges accurately: "What are they of themselves? Institutions of learning? Agents of social mobility? Participants in the welfare system? Contributors to community development? . . . What is their niche? What do they offer that is not provided by other schools? How do their operations differ?"

Although a number of interesting questions are involved, it often seems that one critical issue underlying many discussions of mission is that open door. Apparently questioning the traditional community college commitment to open admissions, Richardson (1981) asks whether it is better to serve everyone at some minimum level or to serve specified constituents at some specified level of excellence? Cosand (1979, p. 3) argues that "the fundamental question the colleges must answer is, Who are the students the college is committed to serve?" Considering the historical contributions of the community college movement, Cross (1979, p. 4) offers this insight: "The community colleges have opened a new frontier in higher education on many fronts, among them open admissions, community involvement, equal opportunity, comprehensive curriculum, and emphasis on teaching. . . . The community college leadership is in a moderate state of disarray today because the new pioneers are not completely sure that the frontier is worth conquering. Thus, before we go much further, we better have some clear idea of what the new frontier is and whether it is worth pushing on against mounting difficulties."

The issues raised pose questions that are critical for planning and program development. While the discussions are conducted in a national forum, it is quite likely that the answers will — and even should — be formulated at the local level. A community college must by definition reflect and promote the interests and needs of its own community. Thus, because communities differ, the missions of local colleges may well also differ.

It is critically important for each college to review and affirm or revise its mission statement as an early and critical step in the strategic planning process (Kieft and others, 1978; Cope, 1978). The mission statement should provide a foundation, a sense of direction, a clearly identified purpose. To plan is not sufficient. The college must first know why it exists.

Using its mission statement as a frame of reference, the college must then establish its goals. When clearly stated goals are tied both to institutional purpose and to the needs of students and community, they provide invaluable criteria for the evaluation of proposals for program and service development and for the allocation of resources to their support. In the absence of goals, the process of program and service development becomes increasingly vulnerable to the criterion of expedience and to the vagaries of institutional politics.

Student Needs and Characteristics

A second cornerstone for program and service development is the institution's understanding of the needs and characteristics of its current and prospective students. While each individual college will have its own unique mix of students, there are several widely prevalent trends that have significant implications for planning.

Student Demographics. The national demographic trends that have the greatest effect on community colleges center on diversification of the population and shifts in the relative representation of age groups. A continuing and highly significant trend in the American population is the aging of the baby boom cohorts; that is, those between the ages of nineteen and thirty-three in 1980 (U.S. Department of Commerce, 1981). Besides having a major effect on school enrollments, this age shift is creating an older work force and a steadily increasing proportion of elderly persons in the total population.

Significant shifts in population characteristics and therefore in student markets have perhaps irrevocably altered the character and mission of the community college. The average age of the community college student, now twenty-eight years, may continue to rise above age thirty. Students older than traditional college age already comprise 40 percent of the community college enrollment (Scully, 1981).

As the numbers of adult students increase, the proportion of part-time enrollments also tends to increase. According to Gilbert (1980), part-time students account for 61 percent of community college enrollments, and the proportion is increasing. Also on the rise is the number of adult female students. The total number of women thirty-five and older enrolled in college has more than doubled since 1972, and the number of part-time women students has doubled each year for the past several years (Project on the Status and Education of Women, 1981).

These very striking trends have led numerous observers to suggest that the primary function of community colleges is to educate adult part-time students (Gleazer, 1980; Zwerling, 1980). If this judgment is accurate — and the statistics seem to indicate that it is — it has tremendous implications for the development of academic programs, instructional methodologies, and student support services. The new adult learners have been characterized as career-oriented, pragmatic, realistic, concerned with economic success, weak in basic skills, and sophisticated in terms of practical life experience (Cross, 1981; Eaton, 1981). Knoell (1976) sees the emergence of students with idiosyncratic objectives who are not interested in one- and two-year programs. Rather, these students will stop in and out of school as they achieve their short-term objectives — or as they discover that their objectives are not being addressed. As Roueche (1980, p. 5) contends, "We must. . . remember that students will not care about learning opportunities unless they see a relevant and useful link between what they need or want to know and what they are being asked to learn."

A proactive approach to the future will require community colleges rigorously to assess their responsiveness to the needs of adult part-time learners. Beside a relevant and useful curriculum, these learners will need counseling, financial aid, childcare, and other services that too often are available only in the daytime or only to full-time students. Those are limitations that most community colleges can no longer afford.

Student Diversity. Community college students have always varied greatly in socioeconomic background, abilities, academic preparedness, age, race, interests, goals, and motivation. Even a cursory glance at projections for future enrollments indicates that the colleges will continue to serve as the point of entry into higher education for diverse types of people: women, middle-aged adults, minorities, immigrants, out-of-school youth, and senior citizens. Thus, it is not surprising that student diversity has emerged as an important issue. In fact, Cross (1980) contends that it is the major issue to be confronted. Cross (1979, p. 9) writes: "As we advance toward the learning society, the frontier that must be conquered is the diversity of the learning force. Unfortunately, the traditional practices of education are totally inadequate as tools for this new frontier."

In addition to their demographic variety, community college students reflect an incredible range of basic skill levels. For example, it is quite possible according to Cross (1979, p. 8) to see a twelve-grade spread (for example, from fourth- to sixteenth-grade level) in mastery of basic skills: "That is not a range that any classroom teacher knows how to deal with, and the situation is going to get much worse as adults from all walks of life enter the learning force." Unfortunately (but not surprisingly), many of the students with inferior basic skills also exhibit a matching deficiency in self-image and confidence in their ability to succeed (Roueche, 1980). Clearly, the challenge posed by student diversity is critical. The community college response to that challenge must be reflected not only in the structure and content of programs and services but also in the professional behaviors and educational methodologies used to implement them.

Community Priorities

As indicated earlier, the community college exists in a unique and reciprocal relationship with its local environment. In the definition of its mission and goals, each individual institution must determine the degree of its commitment to the priorities of its community. If that commitment is serious and substantial, careful assessment of the community's educational needs will be a cornerstone of program and service development. Because communities differ widely, community colleges may serve as cultural centers, or they may emphasize job training, high technology education, or adult literacy programs. Furthermore, community needs are likely to change over time, thereby creating an imperative for the community-oriented institution to exercise vision as well as a certain measure of flexibility. When the local factory closes down, when the community receives a sudden influx of immigrants, or when computer literacy becomes a basic survival skill, the alert community college will often anticipate educational needs and develop or modify programs and services to address them. A number of methods have been successfully used to assess community needs and priorities, including formal surveys, public forums, and advisory committees. These and other available mechanisms are vital in making real the term *community college.*

Involvement of Internal Constituencies

The development of effective programs and services requires participation by affected college groups — faculty, administrators, and students. While cooperation among the different levels of the organization is essential, the development process generally has its focus at the department level. That focus is based on two premises: first, that people who are directly responsible for activities are often best prepared to offer proposals for the future; second, that all plans, however excellent, rely for their success on the persons who must implement them.

With their highly professionalized faculty and their emphasis on academic freedom, institutions of higher education rely heavily on the content expertise of faculty members in the development of academic programs. Proposals are eventually presented to administrators who are responsible for assuring that plans are consistent with overall institutional goals and with goal-related priorities for resource allocation. It is important to remember that program and service development is a value-laden endeavor. One virtue of the participatory process is that it affords an opportunity for the explicit articulation of educational and social values. For example, a new developmental studies program intentionally or unintentionally will reflect the values held by its designers with respect to educational access, individual students, the student-teacher relationship, the utility of learning, the efficacy of certain teaching and learning methodologies, and the importance of students' self-esteem. The role of value judgment becomes even more striking when a collection of proposals for program and service development must be prioritized as part of the budgeting process. Are the needs of students better served by an art history program or by services to displaced homemakers? Is greater benefit provided to the community through an electronics program to support new industry or an English as a second language program created for immigrants in the housing projects? Tenable answers to such difficult questions are best achieved through genuine dialogue among the members of the college community.

Impacts of Technology

During the coming years, technological advances will have far-reaching impact on every aspect of American life. The educational system, including administration, instructional programs, student services, and methodologies for teaching and learning, will be profoundly affected. According to Warmbrod and others (1981), the need for human resource development and training will increase in the areas of technology transfer, robotics, computer literacy, and the general ability to cope with technological change. Community colleges will be called on to serve large numbers of displaced workers who need to learn new technical skills or upgrade existing skills.

However, the impact of technology on instruction will not be limited to the obvious applications in technical education programs. Rather, advances in basic research as well as ever more sophisticated hardware and software will bring technology to the sciences and even to the arts with a steadily increasing pervasiveness. Throughout the institution, impacts will be evident in the content of programs, as the disciplines of high technology (biomedical engineering, for example) are created from the melding or intersection of previously discrete fields of study. But, in addition to the changes in content, instructional tools and delivery systems will be altered by advances in telecommunications, computer-assisted instruction, and computer-managed instruction. New and improved systems will provide individualized, self-paced instruction at times and places convenient to students. Televised instruction and other home-based electronic systems will become increasingly popular.

Although the transition of community colleges into the post-industrial high technology era holds out great opportunity and promise, it will bring serious challenges as well. Madigan and Neikirk (1982, p. 24A) assert that, as brain power replaces muscle power in the American economy, the successful workers will be those who have "a solid basic education, with an emphasis on science and mathematics." However, these authors predict that employers in the growing high technology industries "could find themselves facing a serious labor shortage because of the lack of emphasis on science and mathematics in public education." In that prophecy lies a significant challenge for developers of community college programs.

A further challenge is posed by the high costs for staffing and equipping the high-demand occupational and technical programs. As Cosand (1979) noted, the provision of state-of-the-art training can be extremely expensive, due to the rapid rate at which both personnel and facilities become obsolete. Obviously, sound planning, including needs assessment, labor market analysis, and collaboration with industry, will be critically important.

Toffler (1980) has written about a new technological civilization that is emerging in American life despite widespread efforts to suppress it. Community colleges can ill afford to ignore the implications of technology for college programs and services. To do so would cause them to become irrelevant to their communities and eventually to default to increasing competition from the educational programs developed by business and industry.

Financial Constraints and Political Realities

Last in the list of strategic elements for program and service development are the financial constraints and political realities. While these two elements might seem to be distinct, they are often almost inextricably intertwined, especially in publicly supported institutions. As Cosand (1979, p. 16) states, "the bottom line in any discussion of the future of community colleges is finance," and the colleges depend for their financial support on the state and local political systems.

Like all other public institutions, community colleges have been hurt by inflation, rising personnel costs, and voter resistance to taxation. The remarkable growth of the colleges during the 1960s and 1970s has not been matched by dollars from local, state, and federal governments. Summarizing the forecasts of a number of community college leaders, Breneman and Nelson (1981) predict that college planners will have to contend with continuing inflation, spiraling energy costs, declining productivity, and limited growth in state and local support for higher education. These factors, together with the specter of possible declines in enrollment, are causing a drastic tightening of resources for some community colleges. According to Breneman and Nelson (1980, p. 30), one major result will be an increasing tension between mission and finance, as institutional leaders "will be forced to choose which activities are central to the college and which are of lesser importance."

Funding agencies can be expected to ask tough questions about the mission, quality, and cost-effectiveness of community college education. Community service activities and developmental or remedial programs will be particularly subject to scrutiny. To the extent that they wish to maintain both local autonomy and a comprehensive curriculum, community college leaders and program developers will strive to provide a thoughtful and convincing rationale for the programs and services proposed and offered.

Conclusion

At the outset of this chapter, program and service development was defined as a process through which the community college assesses its changing relationships with its external environment and internal constituencies, then formulates an appropriate pattern of response. Subsequent discussion elaborated on six major strategic elements of that process.

First, program and service development has its roots in a clear statement and affirmation of the institution's mission and goals. Those guiding principles should reflect the achievement of consensus among the college's constituencies about the reason for the institution's existence and the outcomes that it seeks to attain. Second, by examining national trends and conducting its own local inquiries, the college must stay constantly attuned to the needs and characteristics of its current and prospective students. Concurrently with that effort, the college addresses the third strategic element, systematic assessment of community needs and priorities. The educational implications of those priorities will significantly affect the program plans of the community-oriented institution.

Throughout the process of program and service development, the college must take into account a fourth strategic element, the involvement of affected internal groups in development efforts. Only through the open discussion of educational values and priorities can the college hope to arrive at program decisions that ensure quality as well as cooperation in their implementation. Fifth, both the content and the delivery of educational programs will be profoundly affected by the rapid pace of technological development. Finally, proposals for community college programs and services are increasingly subject to the financial and political constraints imposed by an era of reduced resources and increased demands for fiscal and educational accountability.

Given those constraints, the challenges posed to the contemporary community college by the diversity of students, the changing demographics, the transition to a high technology society, and the continuing needs of community college students for basic skills and developmental education can be seen as opportunities to be surmounted. Among educators and others, the term *opportunism* is often applied to the blind pursuit of competitive advantage, with little regard for the fundamental philosophy and purpose of the educational institution. However, the same word also means the art, policy, or practice of taking advantage of opportunities or circumstances. In that sense, program and service development is a form of opportunism. If, as Cope (1978, p. 9) asserts, strategic planning is "opportunity analysis," then program and service development is the means for applying the results of that analysis to the ongoing operations of the institution. It is the process through which colleges can seize opportunities, mold them to the institution's mission, and forge the critical link between goals and action, dreams and reality.

References

Breneman, D. W., and Nelson, S. C. "The Community College Mission and Patterns of Funding." In G. B. Vaughan (Ed.), *Questioning the Community College Role.* New Directions for Community Colleges, no. 32. San Francisco: Jossey-Bass, 1980.

Breneman, D. W., and Nelson, S. C. "The Future of Community Colleges." *Change,* 1981, *13* (5), 16–25.

Cohen, A. M. "Dateline 79 Revisited." In G. B. Vaughan (Ed.), *Questioning the Community College Role.* New Directions for Community Colleges, no. 32. San Francisco, Jossey-Bass, 1980.

Cope, R. G. *Strategic Policy Planning: A Guide for College and University Administrators.* Littleton, Colo.: Ireland Educational Corp., 1978.

Cosand, J. P. *Perspective: Community Colleges in the 1980s.* Horizon Monograph Series. Washington, D.C.: ERIC Clearinghouse for Junior Colleges, American Association of Community and Junior Colleges, 1979.

Cross, K. P. *Adults as Learners: Increasing Participation and Facilitating Learning.* San Francisco: Jossey-Bass, 1981.

Cross, K. P. "Dealing with Diversity." Address to the annual meeting of the American Association of Community and Junior Colleges, San Francisco, March 1980.

Cross, K. P. "The New Frontier in Higher Education: Pioneers for Survival." Paper presented at the Summer Institute of Nova University, San Diego, July 1979.

Drucker, P. F. *Technology, Management, and Society.* New York: Harper & Row, 1970.

Eaton, E. G. "Society 2000: Precedents and Prophecy." *Community and Junior College Journal,* 1981, *52* (1), 6–10.

Gilbert, F. *Two-Year Colleges: Information, Facts, and Figures, 1980.* Washington, D.C.: American Association of Community and Junior Colleges, 1980.

Gleazer, E. G. *The Community College: Values, Vision, and Vitality.* Washington, D.C.: American Association of Community and Junior Colleges, 1980.

Kieft, R. N., Armijo, F., and Bucklew, N. S. *A Handbook for Institutional Academic and Program Planning.* Boulder, Colo.: National Center for Higher Education Management Systems, 1978.

Knoell, D. "Challenging the 'Model and the Myth.'" *Community and Junior College Journal,* 1976, *47* (3), 22–25.

Madigan, C., and Neikirk, B. "High Tech Revolution Hits Work Force." San Antonio *Light,* December 12, 1982, p. 1, 24A.

Martorana, S. V., and Kuhns, E. *Managing Academic Change: Interactive Forces and Leadership in Higher Education.* San Francisco: Jossey-Bass, 1975.

Parnell, D. "Community Colleges in the 80s: A National Perspective." Address to the annual conference of the Association of Texas Junior College Board Members and Administrators, Austin, October 1981.

Project on the Status and Education of Women. *Re-entry Women: Relevant Statistics.* Washington, D.C.: Association of American Colleges, 1981.

Richardson, R. C. Address to the annual conference of the Association of Texas Junior College Board Members and Administrators, Austin, October 1981.

Roueche, J. E. *Holistic Literacy in College Teaching.* New York: Media Systems Corp., 1980.

Scully, M. G. "Volatile Decade Predicted for Community Colleges." *Chronicle of Higher Education,* March 31, 1980, p. 6.

Toffler, A. *The Third Wave.* New York: Morrow, 1980.

U.S. Department of Commerce. *Social Indicators III.* Washington, D.C.: U.S. Government Printing Office, 1981.

Warmbrod, C. P., and others. *Sharing Resources: Postsecondary Education and Industry Cooperation.* Columbus, Ohio: National Center for Research in Vocational Education, 1981.

Zwerling, L. S. "The New 'New Student': The Working Adult." In G. B. Vaughan (Ed.), *Questioning the Community College Role.* New Directions for Community Colleges, no. 32. San Francisco: Jossey-Bass, 1980.

George A. Baker III is executive director of the National Institute for Staff and Organizational Development. He teaches in the Community College Leadership Program at the University of Texas at Austin.

Kay McCollough Moore is assistant to the chancellor of Alamo Community College District, San Antonio, Texas, and a community college planning consultant.

If the top leaders of a college are catalytic figures in ensuring the quality of the strategic vision, indeed, in ensuring that the vision even exists, how can we equip our leaders to design healthy, viable visions?

The Role of the Chief Executive Officer in Strategic Staff Development

Nancy Armes
Terry O'Banion

If having the ability to take the long view as educators and then to make sound strategic decisions is the basis of strategic management, staff development within our colleges needs to provide a framework ensuring that the long view will be taken in such a way as to promote the long-range health of our institution. From this strategic perspective, it may be useful to begin by turning the world of staff development upside down: Strategic staff development and all that the concept implies must be founded on a decision that the program's first priority is to equip top leaders to perform more effectively.

Appropriate to the task and scope of the community college mission, staff development programs have typically been envisioned as embracing all personnel in the college. Nevertheless, most such programs have considered the primary recipients to be faculty. The chief executive officer has been considered the catalytic force in making faculty development programs work by providing authority and resources

G. A. Myran (Ed.). *Strategic Management in the Community College.* New Directions for Community Colleges, no. 44. San Francisco: Jossey-Bass, December 1983.

to underwrite the effort. However, top leaders are not often depicted as primary recipients of the staff development program.

The first beneficiary of a strategically sound staff development program must be the top executives within the institution. Managers and faculty will be clearly tied to the program as it evolves, but not before the president and his or her own needs as a decision maker have been considered. From this perspective, we want to suggest the following scenario for staff development if strategic management is to succeed.

A strategic vision is a clear image of what one wants to achieve in a complex interdependent organization, which then organizes and instructs every staff member to achieve that goal. If the top leaders of a college are the catalytic figures in ensuring the quality of the strategic vision, indeed in ensuring that the vision exists, how best can we equip our leaders to design healthy, viable visions? Misguided vision is not uncommon either in the community college movement or in higher education.

Educators have several obvious handicaps as they visualize the future. First, educational institutions tend to be tradition-bound, and you can never plan the future by the past. But, educators continue to try, even in community colleges. Second, colleges have tended to develop stronger vertical than horizontal alliances. Thus, educators who should have hundreds of resources within the disciplines and programs of their institution are often the last to obtain strategic information. Finally, and perhaps most salient, the pressure on many chief executive officers in our colleges is to demonstrate short-term results. This frequently distorts strategic visioning. Boards, unions, and political structures frequently arbitrate against taking the long view. This particular pressure is perhaps greater among community colleges than it is in the other arenas of higher education.

However, if we assume that it is possible to deal forcefully and successfully with such handicaps, as we must if we are to become strategically healthy, what kind of package will equip today's community college chief executive officer to plan coherently for a future in higher education? The best way to answer that question is by answering two questions: What do we need to know? and What skills do we need to possess?

What the Chief Executive Needs to Know

Today's power to be an effective leader is based in good part on the quality of information transactions that the leader has at his or her disposal. Naisbitt (1982), Yankelovich (1981), the Brookings Institution, the various Carnegie Commissions — these individuals and groups base much of their credibility and the credibility of their recommendations on the quality of the information at their disposal. They devote much professional energy and resources to gathering the most up-to-date information. Only then do they set their considerable collective talents to the task of interpreting.

What categories of information do community college chief executives need in order to lead open-door institutions? Five categories of information seem especially important to community colleges.

The Growing Importance of Science and Technology. Lasers, fiberoptics, and experiments in space; computers, energy management, and genetic engineering — the horizons in science and technology seem virtually limitless. Obviously, many of the scientists and engineers will be trained and later housed in major research universities, but community colleges must assume dynamic leadership in several ways. First, although the engineers may be trained at universities, most of the technicians will be trained at community colleges. There will be three technicians for every engineer, scores of technicians for every scientist.

Second, unless we want the disparity among segments of our society to increase, community colleges must assume great responsibility in making their students literate in areas of science and technology that affect them. Perhaps public education can tackle computer literacy for today's thirteen-year-old or ten-year-old. But, who will work with the forty-year-old, the displaced homemaker, the worker recently laid off? Who will help these adults gain rudimentary knowledge if not the community college?

Finally, many advances in science and technology will affect not only what we teach but how we teach it. The revolution in telecommunications will open classroom doors in brave new ways. The chief executive needs a clear sense of this potential, which may change substantially how we think about the basic issue of access in our colleges. Telecommunications is not the only area that will affect professional methodologies.

The Internationalization of American Life. We already export a third of our agricultural produce, and a third of our American corporate profits come from exports or overseas investments, but the international mobility of capital and production, the enormous international migration of labor, and the dozens of issues related to the allocation and management of resources will become issues that increasingly affect community colleges. As we know, immigrants from around the world already look to community colleges for training; their numbers will grow. Business, industry, and government will increasingly ask us to export curriculum and programs, especially to developing nations, whose coming of age will significantly affect our nation's security.

The Change in the Occupational Structure of American Society. Cetron and O'Toole (1982, p. 15) predict that by the year 2000 there will be almost one million new jobs generated for computer programmers. Other occupations in which demand is predicted to be high include industrial robot technicians, energy technicians, and hazardous waste management technicians. While the titles sound alien, the technologies already exist. If, as has been predicted, robots will displace two thirds of today's factory work force, technology will create enormous training needs that have huge implications for community colleges. This technological revolution will create massive retraining needs as unskilled factory laborers are required to develop new expertise. There is enormous personal pain and national waste in the reality that many individuals are employed in low-wage, dead-end, monotonous work at the very time when skilled worker shortages are dramatically escalating. Community colleges must be at the forefront of training for these huge occupational shifts.

Continuing Demographic Change. In many ways, continuing demographic change seems an old chestnut by now. Still, we must consider the continuing growth of minority populations, the continuing movement from north to south and from east to west, the continuing ramifications of the aging of the baby boom generation, plus demographic trends only beginning to be analyzed intelligently. One such trend is the shift from high-population urban areas to small towns which brings the sophisticated needs and leisure desires of those migrating populations to previously rural and agrarian traditions. From their beginnings, community colleges have been the first among postsecondary institutions to reflect demographic change. This pattern in all likelihood will continue.

Emerging Needs of Human Beings. Community college leaders need to understand the people whom they are going to lead as well as the external events that are occurring. Unfortunately, there will be a tendency to look past these needs, but that is a mistake. A first step is to have access to information about human need as it bubbles up. Sources abound and must be sampled. Naisbitt (1982), Yankelovich (1981), Toffler (1980), and Ferguson (1980) have built their substantial bestseller reputations not only on the hardware of the future but on the shades and texture of human response to change. For example, Yankelovich (1981) describes risk takers who will form personally supportive communities. From another perspective, Naisbitt (1982) describes a phenomenon called *high touch* as a necessary corollary to high technology. For every technological innovation, he attempts to document an equally influential human innovation.

Closer to home, Cross (1981) recently summarized a driving need among community college professionals. Across all strata, these professionals are searching for community, for truly collegial sharing processes in their work environment. If chief executives are to know how to meet such needs as they build strategically, they must pay some attention to behavioral scientists and their popular interpreters, who are making great strides in helping us to understand the human maturation process. To lead human beings, we must first understand them.

What Leadership Skills Are Important

What skills will enable a chief executive officer to assimilate information and plan coherently for the future? Any plan for strategic staff development certainly needs to answer this question and find ways for busy leaders both to develop and to refine the needed skills.

Lesly (1980) speaks eloquently of the masterful managers of past decades — professional managers whose greatest strength was a disciplined mind. These managers focused on facts and realities and abhorred any occurrence that interfered with measurability, predictability, or accountability. Lesly agrees with Toffler that the masterful managers are now doomed, because the leader who is needed in the new, uncertain human climate of our professional worlds is one who can function in ambiguity, constant change, even turmoil. Our centralized, bureaucratic authority figures are no longer adequate, and a new breed must emerge. Naisbitt (1982) speaks of adult work patterns that are decentralized, participatory, alive with networks and multiple options. He describes a changing society that will demand of its leadership openness, the ability to share responsibility, and personal qualities that invite the building of community within a work setting. His vision enables readers to see a spreading of authority, with the typical pattern becoming one of literally hundreds of horizontal work structures that give credibility to a greater number of individuals and that stress the need to listen well.

Maccoby (1981) describes the characteristics most significant in the emerging cadre of successful leaders to be caring, respectful, and responsible attitude; flexibility about people and organizational structure; and the participative approach to management, the willingness to share power. Such leaders are self-aware, conscious of their weaknesses as well as their strengths, concerned with self-development for themselves as well as others.

How does one adapt to the changing workplace and process the incredible amounts of information? What cluster of leadership skills is needed to refine the information and make better use of people as human resources? We have identified four specific skills that leaders already possess but that will need to be further developed and refined during the coming decade.

Listening. If leaders are to be responsive, they must listen well. If Naisbitt (1982) and Yankelovich (1981) are correct and most significant trends within American society are generated from grass roots constituencies, then how well we listen may well determine our survival as viable institutions. Certainly, students, faculty, and community are all speaking more and insisting that their points of view be considered. Although the average adult spends 45 percent of his or her time during a normal day in listening situations, a chief executive officer may find that he or she is more often the speaker than the average person, more called on to iterate than to reiterate, more called on to initiate than to respond. Some of these patterns need to change. Leaders need to listen more. Furthermore, listening to the silent partners within our sphere of influence is just as cogent to a leader as listening to the vocal partners. The president of today's college needs to be able to interpret the unspoken and trace the implications.

Conceptualizing. The strategic thinker must be both comfortable with ideas and able to arrange or rearrange frameworks for his or her ideas. These ideas are a leader's response to information received. The strategic vision that undergirds all long-range planning is the result of strong conceptualizing. Research on the hemispheres of the brain has suggested that our educational systems have tended to value left-hemisphere functions and thus to reward the ability to seek out details, to be analytical. Logically, then, leaders who become Lesly's (1980) masterful managers are those who pay great attention to tying up loose ends. In contrast, encouraging the right hemisphere, which is holistic and pattern-perceiving, becomes more vital if the task of the leader is to anticipate the future.

Collaborating. The skill of working together, talking to one another, sharing ideas, information, and resources is more and more to be valued. Collaboration tends to be cross-disciplinary. It often forms a basis for building personal communities. It signals, through the hard and exhilarating effort of engaging in work with one or more others, that the collaborator is open and willing to grow. Thus, developing personal contacts into collaborations is a skill that leaders should refine. Browning and Johnson (1980), have documented that professionals who share work in collaborative ways have greater resources available to them. Their contacts encourage them to be active rather than reactive; to anticipate danger or coming change because they are an integral part of the grapevine; to better understand hidden agendas; and finally, and perhaps most importantly, to feel a sense of belonging as a result of the nature of their collaborative contacts. Leaders who collaborate learn to give; they learn to be unselfish and to control the megalomania that positional power can encourage.

Self-Understanding. Today's leader must know his or her personal strengths and weaknesses. To plan well for the future, the hard truth is that one must be more open — in a way, more vulnerable. The leader must function much of the time without the secure hierarchical structures that have undergirded so much work of the past. Further, this leader must know where he or she is likely to err and compensate. To be in touch with one's best and worst tendencies is a powerful tool. Since moving strategically is not always popular, self-understanding needs to undergird the leader during difficult times.

Implementation: A Strategy for Gathering Information

After considering both the strategic information and the strategic skills that a leader needs, our scenario must still ask how: How can the information best be gleaned, and how can the skills best be refined for a chief executive officer?

It may be more difficult for presidents of colleges to find professional development than it is for faculty rank and file or mid-level managers in the same institution. Repeatedly, not just in education but in many sectors of the business community, we have encountered executives who were unwilling to reveal their ignorance or to confess their need to develop a certain skill. For example, one outcome of the rapid growth of computer technology is that a whole generation of executives has little specific knowledge of the computer. But, we are told — and it may well be true — if leaders are not willing to assume the role of beginner in this particular arena, they will become cumbersome to the organizations that they seek to lead.

However, it is possible to delineate strategies for professional development for a chief executive officer that are low in threat. Here are several implementation strategies that we value for gathering information: First, it is important to have forums where substantive conversation can occur in an atmosphere of collegiality. Organizations like the League for Innovation in the Community College and the Presidents' Academy sponsored by the American Association of Community and Junior Colleges, as well as a number of professional associations, often provide such forums.

A primary consideration of the League for Innovation in the Community College has been the professional development of chancellors and presidents in the consortium. Two ground rules set the stage for rich professional exchange. First, early on in the league's history, it was decided that the chief executives forming the board of directors could not send a designate to meet in their place. If a president or chancellor could not come, then his college or district would not be represented. Over the years, attendance has been high at these meetings. Obviously, with such a rule, the quality of the peer exchange will not erode. A second ground rule established that membership in the league would be kept small enough that its board of directors could sit comfortably around a common table and exchange ideas in a meaningful way. Thus, the quality of the sharing has not been unduly encumbered by the group's size. The model is a good one. The opportunities for exchange of information are enormous.

Effective use of the computer is another way to gather and control information. The computer will make it increasingly possible for an executive to access huge quantities of information in a selective way. In essence, a leader will be able to devise a system compatible with his or her needs and use computer capability to sift through and call up useful information. It is estimated that every year more than 1,200,000 articles appear in 60,000 books and 100,000 research reports. Until recently, scientific and technical reports have doubled every twenty years. But, during the last decade even that figure has escalated tremendously. Thus, it will become increasingly important to use technology to help us retrieve information.

Another strategy to accomplish the necessary information tasks is for staff supporting the chief executive officer to be capable of capturing, synthesizing, and making accessible useful information on which to base leadership decisions. Here, we would like to suggest the possibility of assigning some of these information-gathering responsibilities to a staff development professional within the institution. Basically, this person becomes a resouce consultant for strategic management. He or she would provide information, offer ways to focus, then find ways to disseminate that information, first to the president, later to other groups within the institution. This person would, in effect, prime college leadership to take the long view. We have developed fairly able systems to track current conditions within our colleges, but we do not always have the power to access information, even in our own colleges, that will in all likelihood affect us in the future. This is the kind of information that a staff development professional could seek out and provide.

Implementation: A Strategy for Skill Building

As for developing appropriate ways for leaders to develop and refine strategic management skills, it may be helpful to envision implementation from two different perspectives. First, there are at least four groups with which a chief executive can and should confer. These need only to be mentioned here because they are widely recognized. Perhaps the key is to see each of these groups as offering opportunities for real exchange and certainly not as groups where the leader must wear a mask afraid to reveal ignorance or lack of skill.

Peer Group. The president must have a group of professional equals with whom he or she can relate as a major source of information. A community college president needs to develop a network with other presidents. This can be done through organizations, it can be through networking at the state level, or it can happen through ongoing contact with presidents who are former graduate school colleagues. Such a peer group is probably the best and most immediate source of relevant information that a president has.

Staff Support Group. The president must not be a lonely leader who operates in isolation. The president who cares about strategic planning will identify and cultivate a core group of key staff members to assist in obtaining information and developing skills. Such staff often include top administrators, whom the president has had a direct hand in hiring, but they probably should also include some key faculty members as well. Such faculty members can be key leaders in the institution, or they can have special skills themselves in the areas needed by the president. Presidents need to take advantage of the human resources in their own institution for developing the skills of listening, conceptualizing, and collaborating.

Board Support Group. Support from the board is an absolute key for the president's long-range survival and creative leadership in the institution. The president who cares about strategic planning will develop a relationship with the board that encourages commitment and involvement among its members with the effective and efficient development of the college. Board members not only provide the essential support needed for long-range planning, they are often wise and experienced leaders who can form another peer group from whom the president can learn, both in terms of information gathering and skill building.

Community Leaders Group. This group is akin to the professional peer group of presidents, but it can be much more diverse and creative. The president who wishes to be effective in long-range planning will develop close bonds with key community leaders to ensure the healthy unfolding of the college's plan. In addition, the president will use these leaders as colleagues in his own continuing development.

Where can such skill development for chief executives be offered? Here are three settings where these opportunities are often provided: Retreats with key staff who are trusted associates can enable the president of a college to plan strategically at the same time that he or she is practicing those listening, conceptualizing, collaborating, and personal growth skills that we have spoken of as requisite skills for strategic leaders. Such retreats, especially if they occur in a retreat setting, can encourage strategic thinking and problem solving.

Work sessions with staff and board members have the potential to develop or refine these skills in leaders. In this case, the dialogue occurs with leaders of the larger community that the college seeks to serve. Since the perspectives are likely to be different, the college leader will once again have to expand his or her information base and enlarge his or her process skills, both of which are valuable outcomes.

On strategic planning days the calendar is cleared, and meetings and telephone calls are discouraged so that thinking, reading, and planning for strategic outcomes can occur. Unfortunately, college presidents are too often consumed by the day-to-day, and the opportunity for long-range planning and strategic consideration goes begging. Leaders have talked about the problem for numbers of years. But, until the chief executive actually makes a commitment to set aside time for strategic planning, such planning for the future will be spasmodic or nonexistent. In the Dallas County Community College District, we made a commitment of this sort during 1982. We set aside two Wednesdays each month for administrators to cultivate visionary skills — to read, think, and plan strategically. On these two days, telephone calls and meetings were discouraged. The response from all administrative levels was positive. Sometimes, the simple and obvious works well.

Developing the Strategic Plan

Ideally, the experienced chief executive will develop a systematic network for gathering information. Such information is crucial for success. Ideally, the chief executive of a major community college will pay attention to developing the skills of listening, conceptualizing, collaborating — skills that make managing and long-range planning come to full fruition. Ideally, most chief executives of community colleges will give considerable attention to the development of a strategic plan for their institution. If they understand their strategic role, they will see themselves as the key to providing leadership for the development of that plan, a plan that will provide clear directions for the college for the next three to five years and that will detail specific activities designed to get there.

In fact, most colleges have a strategic plan, usually developed by internal staff but often with the assistance of outside consultants. These plans speak eloquently of the needs of the community, of the programs to be developed, of the facilities desired, and of the finances needed to support the development of facilities and programs. The plans are often shared with community leaders and staff members and confirmed in a major ritual at a board meeting. But, in too many instances, they cannot be located a year later. Plans have a way of becoming ends in themselves, not a frame of reference for continuing activity over a period of time. Plans often prove to be ineffective, in part because they fail to address two of the most important elements in strategic planning: First, they fail to develop a philosophy explaining how the planners and implementers will work with each other over the life of the plan. Second, they neglect to make a clear statement of staffing requirements, both the kinds of staff needed to implement the plan and the training needed to develop appropriate skills and expertise.

A Staff Philosophy

The college will always have a clear statement of its philosophy and mission indicating basic values and beliefs on which the college is founded and describing fundamental purposes or social roles. Such a philosophy focuses on the larger role of the community college in its community and describes the purpose that the institution plays in helping students to become desirable adults within the community. Most community colleges in the United States have such a statement.

While the statement of this kind of philosophy is important, strategic management calls also for philosophy that provides guidance for how administrators, faculty, and classified staff will interact to achieve the purposes outlined in the statement of mission. This statement sets forth what is believed about how people can work effectively in an institution to achieve broad social goals. Such statements are often understood and practiced informally, but they are seldom articulated as a philosophy to which constituents can openly subscribe. Such statements of philosophy have a way of capturing institutional character, of identifying what makes one community college different from another. Often, this staff philosophy is an extension of the chief executive's own personal leadership style. Such a statement will give character or soul to an institution; when the statement is understood and supported, then a community college emerges as different from the run-of-the-mill community college, as better, even exceptional.

At present, such a statement of staff philosophy is more common among successful corporations in the business world, especially when the corporation has clearly evolved from the personality of its chief executive. The Steak and Ale Corporation, for example, has clearly articulated a corporate philosophy that it uses to recruit staff and by which it expects staff to live. That philosophy was laid down with at least one clear understanding: Any employee not comfortable with it could seek employment elsewhere. In reality, the Steak and Ale philosophy is a set of basic statements that provide direction for all human behavior within the organization:

1. Live by the highest level of integrity and ethics.
2. Set and develop priorities.
3. Be willing to face tough problems.
4. Set and demand standards of excellence.
5. Do what is best for the business.
6. Seek rewards that are worth the risk.
7. Provide clear direction.
8. Keep it simple and direct.
9. Have a sense of urgency.
10. Avoid worrying about things over which you have no control.
11. Be innovative by having the freedom to make mistakes.
12. Be tough but fair with people.
13. Be committed to a quality working environment.
14. Believe in corporate citizenship.
15. Have fun while accomplishing corporate and personal goals.

While it is easier to mandate change in a private corporation than it is in a professional bureaucracy, it is worth noting that the Steak and Ale statement could serve as a standard for community colleges. Indeed, if presented well, it seems likely that this or a similar list of imperatives would become a powerful rallying point, providing substance and behavioral directions for the human beings who must carry out strategic plans in the college. One does not simply assess community needs, define programs, build facilities, and locate finances to support the facilities and programs. Human beings must work together efficiently and effectively in an institution to achieve those goals, and they need a clear statement of expectations from the chief executive that explains how they are to work together in the institution.

Staff Expectations

Once the institution has a philosophy for how it is going to operate on the human level, it becomes relatively simple to outline the kinds of human resources that are needed to make the strategic plan come alive. Using the philosophy as a starting point, the institution's leadership must define the kinds of human resources needed in two categories, new staff who can be recruited and continuing staff who can be developed to achieve the characteristics that the institution needs. From the perspective of the strategic scenario that we are developing in this chapter, only now does the college begin to pay attention to the traditional staff development programs documented in the literature of the past decade.

Assuming that the college is continuing to grow and that it can afford to hire a few new staff members over the next three to five years, careful attention must be given to employing staff members who bring new skills and new creative energies to the task of achieving the mission of the community college. If the strategic plan that has been developed it to be achieved, what new human resources must be added to the institution? We assume that, with only a few new positions to fill and with new and increasingly complex demands being placed on the institution, careful attention must be given to the recruitment and selection of new staff members. If not, it is likely that the strategic plan will be placed in a drawer and forgotten.

The real focus of attention for staff development, however, will be on existing staff members and how they can be provided with opportunities to gather information and develop new skills as implementers of strategic plans. Without detailing how that can be done here, we underscore the value of giving attention to that plan. The chief executive who wishes to realize the strategic plan will not ignore the importance of providing opportunities for faculty and staff to become the kind of people who can implement that plan.

Neither will the chief executive ignore that how he or she encourages renewal will spell defeat or success. This is a key, admittedly pragmatic, reason why the chief executive needs to understand the emerging needs of the human beings who work in the institutional world. Change is not easy, especially among mature adults. Feelings must be attended to. There is an appropriate rhythm. There are rituals that are appropriate to growth. How might a chief executive best call seasoned professionals to new strategic tasks? Here are some guidelines:

First, acknowledge that the first concerns of those whom you would lead in a new direction are almost always personal. (Will it take too much time? Will I be good at it? Will I like it as well?)

Second, look for early adopters — faculty who are likely to try an idea first. In effect, the agricultural extension service model is still alive: Find the farmer who bought the first tractor and teach him new farming methods. Early adopters are leaders. Others will follow.

Third, remember that professionals will internalize training that they can use quickly. Do not open the worlds of telecommunications or information systems if there is no immediate use for such learning on your campus.

Fourth, encourage appropriate support communities. These groups increase the likelihood that a strategic vision will grow at the college. The corporate world speaks of champions — clusters of professionals who steer innovation through the bureaucracy. We need more champions of strategic processes, and since they tend to surface when they have adequate support, it is important to provide an environment where clustering and participation are likely to occur.

Fifth, in the final analysis, strategic development should not be voluntary. The implicit message of a voluntary program is that it is not integral or essential to the health of the institution.

Sixth, strategic staff development should be tied to evaluation. The reasons are obvious. All facets of strategic management have a way of getting lost in the shuffle. There must be operational loops to tie these processes into the day-to-day life of the college.

Summary

If strategic planning is to have a solid base, the role of the chief executive in staff development cannot be overemphasized. The chief executive must be a model. This leader must develop his or her own personal understanding and commit institutional resources to the continuing development of others who will assist in carrying out the strategic plan. The president as strategic planner places priority on people — the people who staff the people's college — and this leader must be keenly aware that he or she is one of those people — in fact, the key person. If the strategic plan is to be a plan of quality and vision and if it is to unfurl in effective and efficient ways, then the president must make his or her own continuing growth and development an essential priority for the college.

101

References

Browning, L., and Johnson, B. "Personal Communities: Networking to Increase Your Impact." *Innovation Abstracts,* 1980, *2* (26).

Cetron, M., and O'Toole, T. "Careers with a Future: Where the Jobs Will Be in the 1990s." *Futurist,* 1982, *16* (3), 11–19.

Cross, K. P. "Community Colleges on the Plateau." *Journal of Higher Education,* 1981, *52* (2), 113–123.

Ferguson, M. *Aquarian Conspiracy.* New York: Houghton Mifflin, 1980.

Lesly, P. "Managing the Human Climate." *Guidelines on Public Relations and Public Affairs,* 1980, *63*.

Maccoby, M. *The Leader: A New Face for American Management.* New York: Simon & Schuster, 1981.

Naisbitt, J. *Megatrends: Ten New Directions Transforming Our Lives.* New York: Warner Books, 1982.

Toffler, A. *The Third Wave.* New York: Bantam Books, 1980.

Yankelovich, D. *New Rules: Searching for Self-Fulfillment in a World Turned Upside Down.* New York: Random House, 1981.

Nancy Armes is special assistant to the chancellor of the Dallas County Community College District.

Terry O'Banion is executive director of the League for Innovation in the Community College.

Sources and Information: Strategic Management

Jim Palmer

To aid readers who seek further information on strategic management, this chapter contains an annotated bibliography of relevant documents processed by the ERIC Clearinghouse for Junior Colleges during the past two years. Items cited in this bibliography deal with institutional responses to change, the role of the administrator in strategic management, budgeting and financial management, and institutional planning. The bibliography concludes with some community college master plans.

   Unless otherwise noted, the full text of these and other ERIC documents can be ordered from the ERIC Document Reproduction Service (EDRS) in Arlington, Virginia, or it can be consulted on microfiche at more than 730 libraries across the country. For an EDRS order form, a list of libraries that have ERIC microfiche collections, or both, contact the ERIC Clearinghouse for Junior Colleges, 8118 Math Sciences Building, University of California, Los Angeles, California 90024.

Institutional Responses to Change

Carroll, C. M. "Educational Challenges of the 80s." Speech presented at the annual conference of the California Community and Junior College Association, Los Angeles, Calif., November 8–10, 1980. 17 pp. (ED 197 801).

G. A. Myran (Ed.). *Strategic Management in the Community College.* New Directions for Community Colleges, no. 44. San Francisco: Jossey-Bass, December 1983.

Discusses a three-part agenda to be followed by California community colleges in response to growing conservatism, dwindling resources, and increasing diversity among students. Calls for greater leadership initiative among presidents, preservation of local control and open admissions, and increased support for basic skills, general education, and other curricular needs.

Koltai, L. *State of the District Address, 1982.* Los Angeles: Los Angeles Community College District, 1982. 18 pp. (ED 225 607).

Suggests means for future district improvement in light of recent and long-term changes in district programs, educational quality, and financial standing. Examines changes in education over the past decade in terms of societal influences, enrollment trends, and skill deficiencies among students.

McCabe, R. H. *Why Miami–Dade Community College Is Reforming the Educational Program.* Miami, Fla.: Miami–Dade Community College, 1981. 7 pp. (ED 211 145).

Examines the response of Miami–Dade Community College to the sometimes conflicting demands of academic excellence and open access. Outlines six directions for college policy that were undertaken to maintain open access while strengthening academic standards.

Moed, M. G. "The Future of Teaching in the Community College." Paper presented at the Conference on the Future of the Community College, New York, N.Y., March 26, 1982. 17 pp. (ED 214 617).

Urges the development of new instructional strategies in response to serious challenges posed by decreased budgets, increased pressures on faculty, and an increasingly heterogeneous student body. Outlines five administrative conditions under which teaching innovation can best occur.

Ramsey, W. L. "New Dimensions in Continuing Education Can Provide Some Concepts for Survival in the 1980s." Paper presented at the College and University System Exchange (CAUSE) national conference, Phoenix, Ariz., December 7–10, 1980. 11 pp. (ED 198 877).

Discusses nine innovative trends in continuing education that have emerged in response to increased demand for nontraditional delivery systems that meet the needs of today's lifelong learner.

Richardson, R. C., Jr. "The Community College in the Eighties: Time for Reformation." Paper presented at the annual convention of the American Association of Community and Junior Colleges, St. Louis, Mo., April 4–7, 1982. 10 pp. (ED 216 723).

Argues that administrators, rather than expanding college missions at the expense of quality, should evaluate the relevance of college activities to the changing external environment. Notes that administrators need to address three key issues in planning: the incompatability and tension between the community services, transfer, and occupational programs; the problem of defining and maintaining educational quality; and the increasing unwillingness of faculty to commit themselves to administratively defined priorities.

Tyree, L. W., and McConnell, N. C. *Linking Community Colleges with Economic Development in Florida. ISHE Fellows Program Research Report No. 3, 1982.* Tallahassee, Fla.: Institute for Studies in Higher Education, Florida State University, 1982, 33 pp. (ED 226 785).

Examines the relationship between business and education in Florida and emphasizes the role of community colleges in fostering economic development. Highlights demographic and economic changes that argue for strong links between education and industry.

Van Groningen, T. "It's Time to Reassess." Paper presented at the annual conference of the Association of California Community College Administrators, Monterey, Calif., March 7–9, 1982. 28 pp. (ED 213 467).

Argues that recent changes in social and cultural values require a reassessment of the mission and function of California community colleges. Urges educational leaders to explore alternatives that will provide greater fiscal stability in the future.

Administrator Role

Griffin, D. F., and Griffin, W. A., Jr. "An 'Ideal' Community College President: A Position Description." Unpublished paper, 1981. 8 pp. (ED 203 946).

Details desirable presidential qualities in terms of personality traits, educational and professional background, and educational philosophy. Outlines general presidential functions in the areas of leadership and college management.

Hall, R. A. *Challenge and Opportunity: The Board of Trustees, the President, and Their Relationship in Community College Governance.* Annandale, Va.: Association of Community College Trustees, 1981. 29 pp. (ED 201 362).

Considers the political context of community college governance; the state's role in governance; the policy-making roles of administrators, trustees, and students; and factors that strengthen the board-president relationship.

LeCroy, J., and Shaw, R. "Community College Leaders for Tomorrow: Emerging Problems and Leadership Strategies to Avert Declining Resources." Paper presented at the annual convention of the American Association of Community and Junior Colleges, St. Louis, Mo., April 4–7, 1982. 15 pp. (ED 216 724).

Examines leadership skills needed by community college administrators to cope with fiscal constraints and shifts in sources of educational finance.

Parcells, F. E. "Role, Duties, and Responsibilities of the Chief Vocational Education Administrator in the Community College." Graduate seminar paper, Southern Illinois University, 1981. 53 pp. (ED 205 229).

Provides a literature review tracing the origins of two-year college vocational education and examines trends in the administration of vocational programs. Identifies the managerial responsibilities of the chief vocational education administrator.

Philips, H. E. "Innovation—What It Is, How to Get It." Paper presented at the annual conference of the Florida Association of Community Colleges, November 11–14, St. Petersburg, Fla., 1981. 9 pp. (ED 211 159).

Defines innovation and discusses managerial tactics to be used by administrators in fostering innovative instructional programs at community colleges.

Ringle, P. M., and Savickas, M. L. "Developing an Environment for Institutional Planning and Management: Setting the Temporal Perspective." Paper presented at the annual convention of the American Association of Community and Junior Colleges, St. Louis, Mo., April 4–7, 1982. 10 pp. (ED 217 916).

Examines the role of the administrator in fostering future-oriented institutional planning. Argues that successful planning depends on the administrator's ability to differentiate institutional events from a temporal standpoint, to view the institution prospectively and retrospectively, to integrate events within a framework of continuity, and to view the future optimistically as something that can be controlled.

Budgeting and Financial Management

Brightman, R. W. "Revenue Diversification: A New Source of Funds for Community Colleges." Unpublished paper, 1982. 24 pp. (ED 221 251.

Argues that community colleges can diversify their sources of revenue instead of reducing or eliminating programs or accepting a decline in quality. Notes that one approach to diversification is college involvement in commercial activities that are undertaken to support educational programs. Examines problems that need to be overcome if such involvement is to be successful.

Clagett, C. A. *Community College Policies for the Coming Financial Squeeze. Working Paper No. 4.* Largo, Md.: Prince Georges Community College, 1981. 41 pp. (ED 205 245).

Presents a metholology used by Prince Georges Community College to assess alternative responses to anticipated fiscal constraints. Enumerates the elements of two policy options: continuing to add new programs as they are needed and implementing a policy of progressive retrenchment. Discusses the steps involved in evaluating each alternative.

Gose, F. J. "Simulating Revenue and Expenditure Limit Projections for a Community College in Arizona." Paper presented at a joint conference of the Rocky Mountain Association for Institutional Research and the Regional Society for College and University Planning, Tucson, Ariz. October 27–29, 1982. 34 pp. (ED 225 605).

Describes a computer model developed at Yavapai College to project changes in college revenue and expenditures over a five-year period. Appendixes provide base figures for the simulation model and a delineation of variables, which include county-assessed valuation and other factors affecting revenue and expenditure limits.

Jacobs, K. J. "Stretching the Educational Dollar." Paper presented at the 1981 Central Region seminar of the Association of Community College Trustees, Osage Beach, Mo., April 12–14, 1981. 17 pp. (ED 205 234).

Notes that trustees have a responsibility to promote cost-effi-
ciency measures and argues that trustees can set an institutional framework for efficiency by asking appropriate questions of administrators
and by remaining informed of college management. Points out that
such measures can alleviate staff fears about reductions and redirect
attention to positive strategies that point to long-term gains.

Kozitza, G. A. *Equity Allocation Model for Multicampus Districts and/or
Large Divisions.* Ventura, Calif.: Ventura County Community College, 1982. 21 pp. (ED 225 614).

Discusses a model to be used in rationally allocating expenditure appropriations among campuses or other college units. Details
steps in the model, which involve the identification of key factors that
are indicative of the need for various expenditure objects. Includes
definitions and illustrative examples.

Loftus, V. L., and others. *Financial Characteristics of U.S. Community
College Systems During Fiscal Years 1977 and 1980.* Normal, Ill.: Illinois
State University, Center for the Study of Educational Finance,
1982. 41 pp. (ED 226 791).

Reports methodology and findings of a study conducted to determine whether a trend (evident from 1950 to 1975) toward increased state
funding, higher tuition, and decreased local support continued during
the latter part of the 1970s. Presents data concerning the financial characteristics of the state public community college systems.

Pickens, W. H. "Managing Fiscal Crisis from the Perspective of a State-
wide Coordinating Agency: The Case of California After Proposition 13." Paper presented at the Conference on Higher Education
Financing Policies: States/Institutions and Their Interaction, Tucson, Ariz., December 4, 1980. 15 pp. (ED 206 342).

Discusses strategies that a state can use in contending with fiscal
problems and turns to California's experiences after passage of Proposition 13 for specific examples. Examines Proposition 13 and its effects
on the revenue base of community colleges.

Scigliano, J. A. "Strategic Marketing Planning: Creative Strategies for
Developing Unique Income Sources." Paper presented at the annual
conference of the National Council on Community Services and
Continuing Education, Danvers, Mass., October 20–22, 1980.
22 pp. (ED 196 474).

Examines the acquisition of alternative funding through the application of marketing strategies that attract new customers and that provide early identification of potential threats to the college, such as community apathy or competition from other institutions. A marketing audit instrument is appended.

Small College Budgeting: A Funding Proposal Prepared by and for Colorado's Small, Public Colleges. Analyst's Technical Report. Denver, Colo.: Colorado State Board for Community Colleges and Occupational Education, 1978. 47 pp. (ED 213 459).

Describes funding and access problems facing small Colorado colleges and examines core activities and appropriations in five budgetary areas: resident instruction, general administrative expenses, student services functions, capital outlay expenditures, and libraries. Summarizes budgetary recommendations and proposed formulas.

Planning the Instructional Program

Arman, H. D. "Community Colleges and Agricultural Education: Strategies for Serving a New Market." Paper presented at the annual conference of the National Council on Community Services and Continuing Education, Detroit, Mich., October 10–13, 1982. 14 pp. (ED 221 256).

Discusses the efforts of Delta College to assess community needs for agricultural programs and examines the college's potential for developing such programs. Describes the development of short-term workshops on diesel engine maintenance, farm building construction, and other topics of interest to local farmers.

Brown, G. C. "Strategic Planning in an Urban Environment: Focus on Education." Unpublished paper, 1982. 9 pp. (ED 216 739).

Reviews the accomplishments of Cuyahoga Community College's Strategic Educational Advisory Committee, a group of eleven administrators and faculty members charged with identifying innovative projects that can be implemented by the college in response to community needs. Discusses four projects recommended by the committee after an analysis of community socioeconomic characteristics and of the college's fiscal, physical, and human resources.

Carling, P. C., and Ryan, G. J. (Eds.). *Report of the 1982 Marketing Committee.* Lincroft, N.J.: Brookdale Community College, 1982. 59 pp. (ED 224 516).

Presents policies, goals, objectives, and activities designed to actualize Brookdale Community College's long-range marketing plan. Includes an outline of a systematic marketing audit.

Eisen, M., and Lucas, J. A. *Feasibility Study for the Establishment of a Human Services Program — Phase II. Volume 12, Number 3*. Palatine, Ill.: William Rainey Harper College, Office of Planning and Research, 1983. 38 pp. (ED 226 804).

Describes a study conducted by William Rainey Harper College to determine the feasibility of establishing a new human services program at the college by assessing the employment opportunities for graduates of the proposed program and the educational needs of persons already employed in the human services field. The questionnaire is appended.

Mehallis, M. V. *Responding to Community Needs Through Community Follow-Up. Junior College Resource Review*. Los Angeles: ERIC Clearinghouse for Junior Colleges, 1981. 6 pp. (ED 202 564).

Presents a literature review examining the utilization of community needs assessment data in program planning and evaluation efforts undertaken by community colleges. Provides citations to additional readings.

Morse, E. *Student Services Planning Model (SSPM)*. Richmond, Va.: Virginia State Department of Community Colleges, 1982. 52 pp. (ED 219 106).

Describes the Virginia Community College System's strategic and operational planning methodology for student services. Presents guidelines for the use of the planning model as well as requisite worksheets, forms, and survey instruments.

Parsons, M. H. "Where Do We Go from Here? The Use of the Market Analysis Survey in Needs Assessment and Program Development." Paper presented at the National Conference, "Needs Assessment: The Pulse of the Community," Blacksburg, Va., May 11, 1982. 16 pp. (ED 217 909).

Argues that market analysis helps to focus program development on identifiable constituencies in the college's service district. Discusses four steps in market analysis and provides instruments used by Hagerstown Junior College in two marketing studies.

Peterson, A. L. *Courses to be Deleted from the Credit and Noncredit Programs of the Community Colleges.* Sacramento, Calif.: Board of Governors of the California Community Colleges, 1982. 11 pp. (ED 217 959).

Describes the procedures used in the preparation of a list of courses to be deleted from the credit and noncredit programs of the California community colleges in response to a $30 million deduction from the total community college apportionment. Examines the effect of course deletions, which affected primarily vocational or personal development courses that could be offered on a self-supporting basis.

User's Guide to Educational Marketing: A Practical Approach for Responding to Community Needs. Portland, Ore.: Portland Community College, 1981. 56 pp. (ED 206 364).

Provides checklists of steps that need to be followed in the development and delivery of new, experimental, and custom-designed programs for the public and private sectors of the local community. Includes a tuition pricing schedule, a sample agreement for contracted services, and sample employment, registration, evaluation, and scheduling forms.

Long-Range Institutional Planning

Arter, M. H. "Use of the Community College Goals Inventory (CCGI) as an Impetus for Change in a Rural Community College." Paper presented at the annual conference of the California Association of Institutional Research, San Francisco, Calif., February 25–26, 1981. 23 pp. (ED 198 861).

Details Palo Verde College's application of the Community College Goals Inventory, which asks respondents to rate the importance of 105 goals in terms of existing and ideal conditions. The goals include outcome goals; process goals relative to student services, accessibility, and other areas; and goals relative to specific college areas, such as parking and childcare services.

Brown, G. C. "Planning for Excellence: A Case Model in a Large Urban Community College District." Unpublished paper, 1982. 10 pp. (ED 216 740).

Discusses the strategy-oriented planning process used at Cuyahoga Community College. Describes how the management functions of planning, leading, and organizing are systematically strengthened through the implementation of an Academic Management System Design and Plan.

Clark, L. R. "An Interactive Planning and Program Evaluation Model for Higher Education." Paper presented at the annual meeting of the North Carolina Association for Institutional Research, Raleigh, N.C., November, 10–12, 1982. 17 pp. (ED 224 515).

Reviews the six phases of the long-range planning model instituted at Western Piedmont Community College in 1982. Includes forms and charts to illustrate various aspects of the planning process, which is designed to clarify issues, establish priorities, achieve consensus on course of action, and allocate resources.

Groff, W. H. "Strategic Planning: A New Role for Management Information Systems." Unpublished paper, 1981. 48 pp. (ED 213 446).

Notes that strategic long-range planning is becoming increasingly dependent on data external to the institution, such as community demographic and socioeconomic characteristics. Examines the concomitant importance of management information systems that are capable of monitoring social changes, assessing institutional strengths, and integrating data concerning the internal and external environments. Includes survey instruments used in strategic planning.

Groff, W. H. "Strategic Planning for Community Services and Continuing Education." Paper presented at the annual conference of the National Council on Community Services and Continuing Education, Detroit, Mich., October 10–13, 1982. 47 pp. (ED 221 249).

Considers the ramifications of the computerized information society for strategic planning and management in community services and continuing education. Presents a conceptual framework concerning the changing nature of society and the implications of this change for postsecondary educational planning.

Kennedy, W. R. "Strategic Planning and Program Evaluation in the Community College." Paper presented at the annual meeting of the American Educational Research Association, Los Angeles, Calif., April 13–17, 1981. 17 pp. (ED 202 506).

Notes the increased need to evaluate programs on the basis of long-term strategic information relating to projected market forces, such as the future economic health of the community or expectations for future state funding. Argues that evaluations based on current budget and enrollment data are no longer adequate.

The Long-Range Plan: "A Plan for the Eighties." July 1982–June 1990. Lenoir, N.C.: Caldwell Community College and Technical Institute, Office of Research and Planning, 1982. 76 pp. (ED 224 530).

Explains the long-range planning process utilized by Caldwell Community College and Technical Institute. Outlines the college's long-range plan as it relates to seven areas: organization and administration, personnel, finance, student development, educational programs, educational development, and facilities. Details objectives, persons responsible, costs, personnel requirements, and equipment requirements for each of the seven areas.

Long-Range Planning Committee Progress Report, 1981–1982. (Vol. 11, No. 15). Palatine, Ill.: William Rainey Harper College, Office of Planning and Research, 1981. 44 pp. (ED 217 930).

Discusses the long-range goals established by a committee that was charged with responsibility for coordinating planning efforts at William Rainey Harper College. Includes minutes of committee meetings, memoranda on a strategic planning workshop, and results of faculty, student, and staff surveys.

Turner, P. M., and others. *Muskegon Community College Long-Range Plan.* Muskegon, Mich.: Muskegon Community College, 1980. 38 pp. (ED 203 952).

Presents long-range planning assumptions and goals for Muskegon Community College as they were submitted by a committee of area citizens. Outlines planning objectives and recommended activities for thirteen areas of concern, including curriculum evaluation, transfer and articulation, staff development, finance, and institutional research and development.

Vaughan, J. L. *Strategic Planning: The Long-Range Future of Community Colleges. A Report by the Projections Committee on Accreditation Reaffirmation at the College of the Mainland. Part I.* Texas City, Tex.: College of the Mainland, 1981. 87 pp. (ED 214 601).

Identifies the principles of strategic planning at community colleges, illustrates the implementation of strategic planning, identifies the conditions conducive to the employment of strategic planning in the college environment, and suggests an organizational framework to facilitate strategic planning.

Institutional Master Plans

Cargol, O. F. *North Idaho College Long-Range Plan and Statement of Institutional Mission and Purpose.* Coeur D'Alene, Idaho: North Idaho College, 1982. 41 pp. (ED 225 611).

States the mission of North Idaho College and specifies goals and objectives to be attained in the next three years. Includes a summary of the basic characteristics of successful college planning, an examination of the results of a needs assessment of college constituents, and an outline of specific objectives for attaining goals in the area of administration, instruction, continuing education, student services, community service, facilities, and finance.

Colvert, C. C. *An Educational Master Plan for Austin Community College.* Austin, Tex.: Austin Community College, 1978. 109 pp. (ED 206 369).

Suggests a master plan for Austin Community College through 1988-89 based on projections of enrollments, finances, and facility requirements.

Occupational Education Master Plan, 1981-1986. Phoenix, Ariz.: Maricopa Community College District, 1981. 87 pp. (ED 210 074).

Presents a five-year master plan to be used by the Maricopa Community College District as a standard against which progress in occupational education can be measured. Discusses underlying assumptions about political climate, the local economy, and other planning factors. Outlines goals and objectives for each of several issues related to the occupational program, including external relations, personnel issues, placement, and the delivery of vocational programs.

Stoehr, K. W., and Covelli, N. J. *Long-Range Plan for Gateway Technical Institute. 1982-1987: Serving Kenosha, Racine, and Walworth Counties.* Kenosha, Wis.: Gateway Technical Institute, 1982. 132 pp. (ED 217 920).

Reviews the socioeconomic situation of Gateway Technical Institute's service district, the institute's mission, projected trends in student enrollment and characteristics, future educational program and support services, and projected financial resources. Discusses the financial and nonfinancial factors that affect the college's long-range plan.

Vancouver Community College Educational Plan, 1980–1985. Vancouver, B.C.: Vancouver Community College, 1980. 150 pp. (ED 212 310).

Presents a five year plan that incorporates nine goals related to the range of college programs, program quality, accessibility, structure, decision making, communication, community relations, support services, and accountability. Examines institutional and market factors likely to affect the 1980–1985 plan.

Jim Palmer is user services librarian at the ERIC
Clearinghouse for Junior Colleges, Los Angeles.

Index

W

Warmbrod, C. P., 82, 86
Washtanaw Community College, shared governance at, 48–49
Wenckowski, C., 67, 73
Western Piedmont Community College, strategic planning at, 112
Wildavsky, A., 64, 73
William Rainey Harper College: program planning at, 110; strategic planning at, 113

Wilson, R., 57–58
Wygal, B. R., 35

Y

Yankelovich, D., 88–89, 90, 92, 101
Yavapai College, financial management at, 107

Z

Zwerling, L. S., 79, 86

Statement of Ownership , Management, and Circulation
(Required by 39 U.S.C. 3685)

1. Title of Publication: New Directions for Community Colleges. A. Publication number: USPS 121-710. 2. Date of filing: 9/30/83. 3. Frequency of issue: quarterly. A. Number of issues published annually: four. B. Annual subscription price: $35 institutions; $21 individuals. 4. Location of known office of publication: 433 California Street, San Francisco (San Francisco County), California 94104. 5. Location of the headquarters or general business offices of the publishers: 433 California Street, San Francisco (San Francisco County), California 94104. 6. Names and addresses of publisher, editor, and managing editor: publisher—Jossey-Bass Inc., Publishers, 433 California Street, San Francisco, California 94104; editor—Arthur Cohen, ERIC, 818 Math Sciences Bldg., UCLA, Los Angeles, CA 90024; managing editor—Allen Jossey-Bass, 433 California Street, San Francisco, California 94104. 7.Owner: Jossey-Bass Inc., Publishers, 433 California Street, San Francisco, California 94104. 8. Known bondholders, mortgages, and other security holders owning or holding 1 percent or more of total amount of bonds, mortgages, or other securities: same as No. 7. 10. Extent and nature of circulation: (Note: first number indicates average number of copies of each issue during the preceding 12 months; the second number indicates the actual number of copies published nearest to filing date.) A. Total number of copies printed (net press run): 1981, 2011. B. Paid circulation, 1) Sales through dealers and carriers, street vendors, and counter sales: 85, 40. 2) Mail subscriptions: 871, 813. C. Total paid circulation: 956, 853. D. Free distribution by mail, carrier, or other means (samples, complimentary, and other free copies): 275, 275. E. Total distribution (sum of C and D): 1231, 1128. F. Copies not distributed, 1) Office use, left over, unaccounted, spoiled after printing: 750, 883. 2) Returns from news agents: 0, 0. G. Total (sum of E, F1, and 2—should equal net press run shown in A): 1981, 2011. I certify that the statements made by me above are correct and complete.

JOHN R. WARD
Vice-President